D1285358

# VERSATILE VENISON

# VERSATILE VENISON

## FROM CAST IRON SKILLETS TO COPPER COOKWARE

### HENRY SINKUS

WILLOW CREEK PRESS®

© 2016 Henry Sinkus

All Rights reserved. No part of this book may be reproduced or transmitted in any form by any means, electronic or mechanical, including photocopying, recording, or by any information storage and retrieval system, without written permission from the Publisher.

Published by Willow Creek Press
P.O. Box 147, Minocqua, Wisconsin 54548

For information on other Willow Creek Press titles,
call 1-800-850-9453

Printed in The United States of America

# TABLE OF CONTENTS

# SOUPS, CHILIS AND STEWS     39

# MISCELLANEOUS — 105

# ETHNIC DISHES

# CHOW MEIN WITH VENISON AND SHRIMP

## SERVES 6

## INGREDIENTS

1 teaspoon salt
1 tablespoon cornstarch
1 cup chicken stock
6 tablespoons vegetable oil
1 pound venison, cut into very thin strips 2 inches long
1 cup raw shrimp, peeled, deveined and cut in half lengthwise
2 carrots, coarsely grated
1 cup raw mushrooms, cut into matchsticks
3 stalks celery, cut thinly on the diagonal
4 scallions, sliced very thin on the diagonal
4 tablespoons teriyaki sauce
4–6 cups medium noodles (about 8 ounces uncooked fettuccine noodles)

## DIRECTIONS

Mix the salt and cornstarch with the chicken stock.

Set a large wok or sauté pan over high heat for 30 seconds. Add 3 tablespoons of vegetable oil and wait until it begins to smoke. Add the venison and stir-fry for 2 minutes. Add the shrimp and continue cooking for 1 minute more.

Add the carrots, mushrooms, celery, scallions and teriyaki sauce. Stir-fry for 3 minutes. Pour in the cornstarch mixture and stir until thickened. Adjust seasoning with additional salt and teriyaki if desired.

In a large skillet, heat the remaining 3 tablespoons of vegetable oil over medium heat. Add the cooked noodles and stir until heated through. Transfer noodles to a serving bowl and top with the venison/shrimp mixture.

## HENRY SAYS: HEAT LEFTOVERS FOR LUNCH AND SERVE ON A HAMBURGER BUN—YOUR NOT-SO-TRADITIONAL CHOW MEIN SANDWICH.

# IRISH VENISON LOAF

## SERVES 6–8

## INGREDIENTS

2 tablespoons butter
1 teaspoon vegetable oil
1 medium onion, minced
1 pound ground venison
½ pound ground beef
¼ pound bulk pork sausage
1 clove garlic, minced
½ teaspoon white pepper
1 teaspoon ground nutmeg
2 eggs, lightly beaten
dash Tabasco
¾ cup seasoned breadcrumbs
1 cup Parmesan cheese, grated
2 teaspoons Dijon mustard
1 tablespoon ketchup
¼ teaspoon oregano, crumbled

## DIRECTIONS

Preheat oven to 375 degrees. Heat butter and oil in a medium saucepan. Sauté the onion until transparent. Remove from heat.

In a large bowl, thoroughly combine the venison, beef, sausage, garlic, pepper and nutmeg. Add the eggs, Tabasco, breadcrumbs and ½ cup of cheese.

Shape mixture into a loaf in a shallow baking dish. Combine the mustard, ketchup and oregano, and spread over the loaf. Bake for 1 hour. Remove from oven and sprinkle top with remaining ½ cup of Parmesan cheese. Bake 15 minutes longer. Remove from oven and let stand for 10 minutes before slicing.

## HENRY SAYS: IF IT'S IRISH, IT HAS TO BE STEAMED POTATOES AND CARROTS.

# ITALIAN VENISON MEATBALLS

## SERVES 4–6

## INGREDIENTS

1 pound ground venison
1 pound bulk sweet Italian sausage
1 15 ounce can stewed tomatoes, drained and finely chopped
½ cup Italian Panko bread crumbs
½ cup white cheddar cheese, shredded
¼ teaspoon granulated garlic
¼ teaspoon celery salt
2 tablespoons Italian salad dressing
2 eggs, beaten
1 24 ounce jar of your favorite pasta sauce

## DIRECTIONS

Preheat oven to 350 degrees. In a large bowl, combine the venison, sausage, tomatoes, bread crumbs and cheese. Add the granulated garlic and celery salt, and mix well. Shape into 36 to 40 meatballs.

Place the meatballs on racks in nonstick baking trays and bake for 20 to 30 minutes, or until internal temperature reaches 130 degrees. Remove from oven.

Place the meatballs in a baking dish, cover with the pasta sauce and bake for 15 minutes at 325 degrees. Serve over your favorite pasta.

HENRY SAYS: TO FREEZE LEFTOVERS FOR LATER USE, LINE BAKING TRAYS WITH WAXED PAPER. ARRANGE THE SAUCED MEATBALLS IN A SINGLE LAYER ABOUT ½ INCH APART AND FREEZE ABOUT 6 HOURS. PLACE THE INDIVIDUALLY FROZEN MEATBALLS AND SAUCE IN GALLON ZIP-LOCK BAGS AND STORE IN THE FREEZER. WHEN YOU'RE READY TO USE THEM, TAKE OUT AS MANY AS YOU NEED, DEFROST THEM, PLACE IN A BAKING DISH, COVER AND BAKE AT 325 DEGREES FOR 20 MINUTES. VOILA—DINNER'S READY!

# ITALIAN VENISON

## INGREDIENTS

2 pounds venison, cut into bite-sized pieces
¼ teaspoon black pepper
½ teaspoon oregano
¼ teaspoon salt
2 cloves garlic, minced
1 tablespoon brown sugar
2 24 ounce jars of your favorite pasta sauce
2 green peppers, seeded and chopped
2 medium onions, chopped
½ cup Parmesan cheese, grated

## DIRECTIONS

Add all ingredients to a large Dutch oven and mix well. Cover and simmer over low heat 2 to 3 hours, or until venison is tender. Check every 30 minutes and add water as necessary. Serve over pasta and top with Parmesan cheese.

HENRY SAYS: ITALIAN FOOD ISN'T ITALIAN WITHOUT CHEESE AND WINE, SO DON'T FORGET THE CHIANTI.

# LITHUANIAN VENISON AND KIELBASA LOAF

## SERVES 4–6

### INGREDIENTS

4 tablespoons butter
8 slices thick-cut bacon, chopped
1 large onion, chopped
1 large green pepper, chopped
2 cloves garlic, minced
1 cup rye bread crumbs
½ cup cream
2 eggs
2 teaspoons sweet Hungarian paprika
¼ teaspoon white pepper
1 teaspoon seasoned salt
2 pounds ground venison
½ pound kielbasa, sliced ¼ inch thick and cut in half
1 cup sour cream

### DIRECTIONS

Preheat oven to 350 degrees. Melt the butter in a large saucepan. Add the bacon, onion, green pepper and garlic, and cook over medium heat until the onion begins to brown, 6 to 8 minutes. Remove from heat.

In a large bowl, combine the bread crumbs, cream, eggs, paprika, salt and pepper. Add the venison, kielbasa, bacon and onion mixture, and blend well. Pack mixture into a 9x5x3 inch loaf pan and bake 1 hour, or until internal temperature reaches 160 degrees. Allow loaf to cool 15 minutes before slicing.

## HENRY SAYS: SERVE WITH SOUR CREAM AND SAUERKRAUT FOR A REAL TASTE OF LITHUANIA.

# SWEET SOUR VENISON

## INGREDIENTS

2 pounds venison, sliced ½ inch thick and cut into ¼ inch strips
¼ cup cornstarch
⅓ cup teriyaki sauce
2 tablespoons vegetable oil
1 green bell pepper, seeded and cut into strips
1 medium onion, sliced and cut in half
2 medium carrots, sliced diagonally
1 tablespoon cornstarch
2 tablespoons sugar
2 tablespoons ketchup
¼ cup teriyaki sauce
2 tablespoons lemon juice
⅛ teaspoon toasted sesame seeds
½ tablespoon sesame oil
1 8 ounce can pineapple chunks, drained

## DIRECTIONS

In a medium size bowl, whisk together the ¼ cup cornstarch and ⅓ cup teriyaki sauce. Add the venison and toss to coat. Let sit at least 5 minutes.

In a wok or large skillet, heat the oil. Remove the venison from the marinade with a slotted spoon and stir-fry until brown. Remove venison from the wok. Stir-fry the vegetables for 3 to 5 minutes, or until tender crisp. Return the venison to the wok. Whisk together 1 tablespoon cornstarch, sugar, ketchup, lemon juice, ¼ cup teriyaki sauce, sesame seeds and sesame oil. Add to venison mixture in the wok and simmer for 3 to 5 minutes, or until thickened. Stir in the pineapple and heat until bubbly. Serve over steamed white or brown rice.

HENRY SAYS: ADD A FEW DROPS OF
TABASCO TO HEAT UP THE SAUCE.

# SZECHUAN VENISON, NOODLES AND CABBAGE

## SERVES 4–6

### INGREDIENTS

1 pound ground venison
1 tablespoon vegetable oil
2 tablespoons fresh ginger, minced
2 shallots, thinly sliced
½ tablespoon Chinese five spice powder
3 tablespoons teriyaki sauce
1 small head napa cabbage, thinly sliced
1 teaspoon sesame chili oil
1 cup chicken stock
12 ounces noodles, cooked (like linguini or spaghetti)
2 scallions, sliced thinly on the diagonal

### DIRECTIONS

In a large sauté pan, heat the vegetable oil over medium heat. Add the venison and stir until slightly browned.

Add the ginger, shallots, five spice powder, teriyaki and cabbage. Cook 4 to 5 minutes. Add the sesame oil, chicken stock and cooked noodles. Cover and reduce heat to low. Simmer until the noodles are hot. Garnish individual servings with sliced scallions.

## HENRY SAYS: IF YOU'D LIKE MORE HEAT, ADD ¼ TEASPOON CRUSHED RED PEPPER AND 1 TEASPOON BROWN SUGAR.

# TEXICAN VENISON MEATBALL SOUP

## SERVES 6–8

## INGREDIENTS

2 tablespoons olive oil
1 large onion, chopped
2 medium carrots, chopped
2 medium zucchini, chopped
2 cloves garlic, minced
2 tablespoons canned chopped green chiles
4 cups beef broth
2 14 ounce cans stewed tomatoes, coarsely chopped
1 teaspoon marjoram
½ teaspoon ground cumin
¼ teaspoon pepper
1 cup frozen corn
¼ cup instant rice
1 egg
2 tablespoons cilantro, chopped
2½ teaspoons chili powder
1 teaspoon salt
1 pound venison, ground
½ pound bulk pork sausage

**HENRY SAYS: SERVE WITH CORN CHIPS AND HAVE SRIRACHA SAUCE ON HAND FOR THOSE WHO LIKE IT HOT!**

## DIRECTIONS

In a large non-reactive Dutch oven, heat the olive oil over medium heat. Add the onion, carrots, zucchini, garlic and green chiles. Cover and cook, stirring occasionally, until the vegetables are softened, 8 to 10 minutes.

Add the beef broth, tomatoes with the liquid, marjoram, cumin and pepper. Bring to a simmer, reduce heat to low and cook for 1 hour. Stir in the corn.

In a medium saucepan, cook rice in boiling water for 5 minutes. Drain the rice and rinse twice under cold water.

In a medium bowl, combine the rice, egg, cilantro, chili powder and salt with a fork. Add the venison and pork sausage and mix well. Form this mixture into 1 inch meatballs and drop into the soup. Increase the heat to high and return to a simmer. Reduce heat to low, partially cover the pot and simmer, stirring gently, until meatballs are cooked through, 15 to 20 minutes.

# THAI VENISON AND RICE SOUP

## SERVES 4–6

### INGREDIENTS
1 pound coarsely ground venison
5 slices finely chopped thick-cut bacon
1 egg
4 cups chicken stock
2 cups cooked rice
2 tablespoons fish sauce
4 finely shredded lettuce leaves
3–4 slices peeled fresh ginger, minced
3 finely sliced green onions
¼ teaspoon white pepper
to taste brown sugar
to taste teriyaki sauce

### DIRECTIONS
Mix together the ground venison, bacon and egg. Form into ¾ inch balls.

In a large saucepan, bring the chicken stock to a boil over medium heat. Reduce heat to low and carefully add the venison meatballs. Simmer until firm and cooked through (about 6 to 8 minutes).

Add the rice, fish sauce, lettuce, ginger, green onion and white pepper. Simmer for an additional 5 minutes. Season to taste with brown sugar and teriyaki sauce.

## HENRY SAYS: HEAT THIS SOUP UP WITH ½ TEASPOON OF RED CURRY PASTE.

# VENISON CURRY

## SERVES 6–8

## INGREDIENTS

2 teaspoons minced garlic
2 tablespoons yellow curry powder or paste
1½ tablespoons brown sugar
⅓ cup teriyaki sauce
3 tablespoons vegetable oil
2 pounds venison, cut into thin strips 2 inches long
1 package pre-cut butternut squash
2 large onions, thickly sliced and cut in half
2 medium potatoes, peeled and cut into 1 inch dice
1 package cabbage slaw mix
1 tablespoon ginger, peeled and finely minced
1 cup baby carrots, cut into thirds
3 cups chicken stock
4 tablespoons rice wine
1 tablespoon cornstarch mixed with ¼ cup rice wine
1 16 ounce can coconut milk

## DIRECTIONS

In a medium bowl, combine the garlic, curry, brown sugar and teriyaki sauce. Add the venison and toss to coat. Marinate at least one hour.

Heat the oil in a large Dutch oven over medium high heat. Stir-fry the venison in several batches until browned but not crispy. Reduce heat to medium. Place all venison back in the Dutch oven. Stir in the squash, onions and potatoes. Cook until the onions are soft, about 10 minutes. Add the cabbage slaw, ginger, baby carrots, chicken stock and rice wine. Stir to combine well. Cover and cook until vegetables are tender, about 30 minutes.

Stir in the rice wine/cornstarch mixture. Bring to a boil. Reduce to simmer and add the coconut milk. Serve over rice.

## HENRY SAYS: I GENERALLY USE JASMINE RICE—IT HAS A WONDERFUL AROMA AND ADDS A DELICIOUS FLOWERY FLAVOR TO THE CURRY.

# VENISON SCHNITZEL

## SERVES 6–8

## INGREDIENTS

6–8 venison leg slices, cut ½ inch thick
4 cups Ritz Cracker crumbs
3 large eggs, beaten
3 tablespoons butter
3 tablespoons olive oil

## DIRECTIONS

Preheat oven to 350 degrees.

Place leg slices (one at a time) between 2 sheets of wax paper and flatten to ¼ inch with a kitchen mallet. This will take a while.

Place the cracker crumbs in a large pie plate next to a shallow bowl with the beaten eggs. Have a tray close by. Dip the venison in the egg, then coat completely with the cracker crumbs and lay in a single layer on the tray.

Heat half of the butter and half of the olive oil in a large skillet over medium-high heat. Fry 2 to 3 schnitzel at a time, browning well on each side. Transfer to a baking pan in the oven when done to keep warm. Add more butter and olive oil to the skillet as required and complete this process until all of the venison is cooked.

## HENRY SAYS: SERVE WITH SPAETZLE AND SWEET AND SOUR RED CABBAGE. HOW ABOUT APPLE STRUDEL FOR DESSERT?

# WONTONS

## 16 WONTONS

## INGREDIENTS
½ pound ground venison
2 strips pre-cooked bacon, minced
1 large shallot, finely minced
1 teaspoon sweet Oriental chili sauce
16 wonton wrappers
3 cups vegetable oil

## SAUCE
¼ cup teriyaki sauce
¼ cup rice wine
1 scallion, thinly sliced on the diagonal

## DIRECTIONS
In a medium bowl, mix together the venison, bacon, shallot and chili sauce. Place 1 teaspoon of this mixture on the center of each wonton wrapper. Moisten the edges of the wrapper and bring the 4 corners to the center and pinch to seal.

Heat vegetable oil over medium heat in a large saucepan until bubbles form around the handle-end of a wooden spoon dipped in the oil. Fry wontons until golden brown on all sides. Drain on paper towels.

Combine all sauce ingredients for rice wine sauce.

## HENRY SAYS: SOME PREFER TO OMIT THE FILLING ALTOGETHER AND SIMPLY CUT THE WRAPPERS INTO STRIPS, FRY THEM AND SERVE WITH A SWEET AND SOUR SAUCE.

# MEATLOAF, MEATBALLS

# CHEESY VENISON MEATLOAF

## SERVES 4–6

### INGREDIENTS
1 clove garlic, minced
1 cup cheese crackers, crushed
1 egg, beaten
1 can cheddar cheese soup
1½ pound ground venison
1 pound raw Polish sausage, casing removed
1 cup mild cheddar cheese, shredded

### DIRECTIONS
Preheat oven to 350 degrees. In a medium bowl, combine the garlic, crackers, egg and half of the soup. Let stand for 10 minutes. Add the venison sausage and cheese and mix well.

Pack into a 9x5x3 inch loaf pan, place on a baking tray and bake about 40 minutes or until thermometer inserted in the center reads 130 degrees. Pour remaining soup over the meatloaf, return to the oven and bake until thermometer reaches 160 degrees. Let stand 10 minutes before serving.

## HENRY SAYS: THIS MEATLOAF CRIES OUT FOR MASHED POTATOES.

# COCKTAIL VENISON MEATBALLS

## 48 MEATBALLS

## INGREDIENTS

2 pounds ground venison
1 pound bulk Italian sweet sausage
1 cup grated Parmesan cheese
2 eggs, beaten

## SAUCE

1 jar currant jelly
1 cup barbecue sauce (your choice)

## DIRECTIONS

In a large bowl, combine the venison, sausage, cheese and eggs, mixing well.
Form into 1 inch meatballs.

Place meatballs in a non-stick pan and bake in a 350 degree pre-heated oven for 20 to 30 minutes or until cooked through.

For the sauce, combine the jelly and barbecue sauce in a medium saucepan and cook, stirring constantly, over medium heat until the jelly is melted.

Pour the sauce over the meatballs.

HENRY SAYS: GET CREATIVE WITH YOUR CHOICE OF BARBECUE SAUCE—MAYBE A LITTLE SMOKINESS, SOME BOURBON FLAVOR, SWEET AND SOUR... WHATEVER TRIPS YOUR TRIGGER.

# HAM AND VENISON MEATBALLS

## SERVES 4–6

## INGREDIENTS
1 cup Panko bread crumbs
1 cup buttermilk
¼ teaspoon salt
¼ teaspoon black pepper
2 tablespoons butter
1 small onion, minced
1 medium green bell pepper, minced
1 clove garlic, minced
1 egg, beaten
1½ pounds ground venison
½ pound ham, ground or minced
1 package hollandaise sauce mix, prepared with milk and butter

## DIRECTIONS
Preheat oven to 325 degrees. In a medium bowl, combine the bread crumbs, buttermilk, salt and pepper. Let stand 15 minutes.

Melt the butter in a medium saucepan over low heat. Add the onion, green pepper and garlic, and stir until the vegetables are softened. Cool about 5 minutes. Add to the buttermilk and bread crumb mixture. Stir in the egg, venison and ham, mixing well.

Form into approximately 30 meatballs and place on a non-stick baking tray. Bake for 15 to 18 minutes. Transfer to a heated serving dish and garnish with the hollandaise sauce.

## HENRY SAYS: THIS DISH GOES PERFECTLY WITH A GREAT BIG BOWL OF WIDE EGG NOODLES.

# HEARTY VENISON MEATLOAF

SERVES 4–6

## INGREDIENTS

1½ cups Bran Flakes, crushed
2 eggs
1 cup tomato salsa
1 medium onion, chopped
1 medium green bell pepper, chopped
2 cups corn
1½ teaspoons garlic salt
¼ teaspoon pepper
2 pounds ground venison
½ pound thick-cut bacon, chopped
⅓ cup ketchup

## DIRECTIONS

Preheat oven to 350 degrees. In a large bowl, mix the Bran Flakes, eggs, salsa, onion, green bell pepper, corn, garlic salt and pepper. Add the ground venison and bacon. Mix with your hands until completely blended. Place in a greased 8x4 inch loaf pan.

Place on a baking sheet and bake, uncovered, until a meat thermometer in the center of the loaf reads 160 degrees, approximately 1 hour. During the last 15 minutes of baking, spread the ketchup over the top of the meatloaf. Remove from the oven and let stand for 5 minutes before slicing.

## HENRY SAYS: TASTES GREAT AND GOOD FOR YOU!

# LEFTOVER VENISON MEATLOAF AND POTATO PIE

## SERVES 4–6

## INGREDIENTS

1 4.2 ounces carton dehydrated hash brown potatoes (re-hydrated according to package instructions)
4 eggs, beaten
2 cups leftover venison meatloaf, crumbled
¾ cup sharp cheddar cheese, grated
4 green onions, thinly sliced
½ teaspoon salt
½ teaspoon smoked paprika

## DIRECTIONS

Preheat oven to 375 degrees. In a large bowl, combine all ingredients and mix well.

Butter a deep 10 inch pie pan and add the mixture. Bake 30 to 40 minutes until the top is golden brown and the pie is completely set. Remove from the oven and let sit for 10 minutes before serving.

## HENRY SAYS: TO GIVE THIS DISH A TEX-MEX FLAVOR, SERVE WITH SOUR CREAM AND SALSA.

# MARTY'S VENISON MEATBALLS

## 30 MEATBALLS

## INGREDIENTS
3 cups beef broth
2 tablespoons red currant jelly
2 tablespoons hot pepper jelly
2 tablespoons mild salsa


1 cup Kalamata olives, pitted
1 large shallots, chopped
½ cup fresh mint leaves
¾ cup fresh flat-leaf parsley
¾ cup Italian Panko bread crumbs
½ cup ricotta cheese
3 egg yolks
1 teaspoon sea salt
½ teaspoon freshly ground black pepper
1 pound ground venison
1 pound bulk sweet Italian sausage

## DIRECTIONS
Preheat oven to 425 degrees.

In a 1½ quart saucepan, bring the beef broth to a boil over medium-high heat. Reduce heat to low, stir in the jellies and salsa, cover and remove from heat.

Fit the bowl of a food processor with the chopping blade. Add all remaining ingredients, except the venison and Italian sausage. Pulse/chop until completely incorporated. Add the venison and Italian sausage and pulse/chop until well blended. Form into 1 inch meatballs and place on a non-stick baking pan. Bake for 15 minutes. Transfer to a serving dish and top with the sauce.

## HENRY SAYS: THESE MEATBALLS ALSO MAKE A GREAT APPETIZER.

# MY MOTHER'S VENISON MEATLOAF

## SERVES 4–6

## INGREDIENTS

1 medium onion, chopped
2 eggs
⅔ cup oatmeal
½ cup ketchup
1 tablespoon Worcestershire sauce
1 teaspoon salt
¼ teaspoon pepper
1 pound ground venison
1 pound bulk pork sausage
3 tablespoons ketchup

## DIRECTIONS

Preheat oven to 375 degrees. In a medium bowl, combine the onion, eggs, oatmeal, ½ cup ketchup, Worcestershire sauce, salt and pepper. Add the venison and pork sausage, and blend well.

Place mixture in an 8x4 inch loaf pan. Place on a baking sheet and bake, uncovered, for 45 minutes. Spread the remaining 3 tablespoons of ketchup over the top of the meatloaf and bake until a meat thermometer in the center of the loaf reads 160 degrees, approximately 15 minutes longer. Remove from the oven and let stand for 5 minutes before slicing.

## HENRY SAYS: MY MOTHER WOULD CALL THIS HER "DEPRESSION MEATLOAF."

# SOUTHWESTERN VENISON MEATLOAF

SERVES 4–6

## INGREDIENTS
1 cup tomato salsa, drained
1 cup tortilla chips, finely crushed
1 egg
1 small onion, chopped
1 clove garlic, minced
1 small fresh green chile, seeded and minced
1 tablespoon chili powder
1 teaspoon celery salt
½ teaspoon ground cumin
2 pounds ground venison
½ pound thick-cut bacon, diced
½ cup sharp cheddar cheese, shredded

## DIRECTIONS
Preheat oven to 375 degrees. In a medium bowl, combine the salsa, tortilla chips, egg, onion, garlic, chili powder, celery salt and cumin. Mix well. Add the venison and bacon, and mix until blended.

Place mixture in an 8x4 inch loaf pan. Place on a baking sheet and bake, uncovered, until a meat thermometer in the center of the loaf reads 160 degrees, approximately 1 hour. Sprinkle the cheddar cheese over the top of the meatloaf and bake until cheese is melted, approximately 3 minutes. Remove from the oven and let stand for 5 minutes before slicing.

HENRY SAYS: TO BRIGHTEN UP THIS DISH,
SERVE WITH A BOWL OF SALSA ON THE SIDE.

# SWEET AND SOUR VENISON MEATBALLS

## SERVES 4–6

## INGREDIENTS

1 egg, beaten
1 cup soft bread crumbs
1 small onion, minced
2 tablespoons milk
¾ teaspoon salt
2 pounds ground venison
½ pound fresh bulk pork sausage
2 tablespoons butter
1 8 ounce can crushed pineapple
1 8 ounce can whole cranberry sauce
½ cup barbecue sauce
¼ teaspoon salt
dash black pepper
1 tablespoon cornstarch
¼ cup cold water
½ cup green pepper, cut into strips

## DIRECTIONS

In a large bowl, combine egg, bread crumbs, onion, milk and ¾ teaspoon salt. Add venison and pork sausage and mix well. Shape into one-inch meatballs.

In a large skillet, melt the butter and brown the meatballs over medium heat. Drain off any excess fat.

Drain the pineapple, saving the syrup. In a small bowl, combine the syrup, cranberry sauce, barbecue sauce, ¼ teaspoon salt and pepper. Pour over the meatballs in the skillet. Bring to a boil and reduce heat to low. Cover and simmer 15 to 20 minutes.

Combine cornstarch and cold water in a small bowl. Add to the skillet, stirring well and cook, stirring constantly, until thickened. Add the pineapple and green pepper. Simmer covered until pepper is barely tender. Serve over rice.

## HENRY SAYS: THESE MEATBALLS CAN ALSO BE SERVED AS AN APPETIZER.

# VENISON LOAF FROM THE WATERS

### SERVES 4–6

## INGREDIENTS

2 cups chicken broth
½ cup wild rice
2 cloves garlic, minced
3 stalks celery, finely sliced
1 medium onion, chopped
1 medium carrot, shredded
2 eggs
½ cup cream
½ cup craisins, soaked in 1 cup red wine for 1 hour and drained
½ cup seasoned bread crumbs
8 slices pre-cooked bacon, chopped
¼ cup fresh parsley, chopped
½ teaspoon basil
½ teaspoon oregano
1 teaspoon salt
¼ teaspoon white pepper
2 pounds ground venison

## DIRECTIONS

In a medium saucepan, bring the chicken broth to a boil. Stir in the wild rice, reduce heat to low and cover. Simmer until the rice blooms and is tender, 50 to 60 minutes. Drain liquid from the rice and discard.

Preheat oven to 350 degrees. In a large bowl, combine the garlic, onion, carrot, eggs, cream, drained raisins, bread crumbs, bacon, parsley, oregano, basil, salt and pepper. Add the venison and mix well. Pack into a greased 9x5x3 inch loaf pan. Bake until the internal temperature reaches 160 degrees, approximately 1 hour. Let stand 10 minutes before slicing.

## HENRY SAYS: SERVE WITH CURRANT JELLY AND OVEN-BAKED POTATOES.

# VENISON MEATBALL PIE

## SERVES 4–6

## INGREDIENTS

1 package refrigerated piecrust dough
20 Italian meatballs, thawed (from recipe on page 27)
¼ cup flour
1 medium potato, cut into ¼ inch dice
1 15 ounce can peas and carrots, drained
1 15 ounce can whole-kernel corn, drained
1 small green pepper, diced
1 large onion, thinly sliced
2 cans vegetable soup
½ cup ketchup
¼ teaspoon granulated garlic
2 tablespoons Worcestershire sauce
salt & pepper to taste

## DIRECTIONS

Preheat oven to 375 degrees. Roll out piecrust dough to fit your 10 inch pie plate and place in the plate.

Dust the meatballs lightly with flour and arrange in the pie plate. Add the potato, peas and carrots, corn and green pepper. Top with the onion.

In a medium bowl, combine the soup, ketchup, granulated garlic and Worcestershire sauce. Mix well, season with salt and pepper to taste and pour over the ingredients in the pie plate.

Roll out the second piecrust dough and place on top of the pie. Crimp all around the edges and cut several vents in the top. Place on a sheet pan and bake for 30 to 40 minutes, or until top is golden brown. Remove from oven and cool for 15 minutes before serving.

## HENRY SAYS: A FRESH SALAD, A GENEROUS PIECE OF PIE—A MEAL TO REMEMBER!

# VENISON MEATLOAF AND PAN GRAVY

SERVES 6–8

## INGREDIENTS

1 large onion, finely chopped
1 large green bell pepper, finely chopped
2 eggs
¾ cup oatmeal
½ cup tomato sauce
2 tablespoons steak sauce
¾ teaspoon garlic salt
¼ teaspoon pepper
2 pounds ground venison
1 pound bulk pork sausage
3 tablespoons butter
1 tablespoon flour
2 cups chicken stock
1 cube beef buillion
2 cups milk
salt & pepper to taste

HENRY SAYS: FOR AN EXTRA SPECIAL MEAL ADD ½ CUP CRAISINS TO THE MEATLOAF AND SUBSTITUTE CREAM FOR THE MILK IN THE GRAVY. SERVE WITH MOUNDS OF CREAMY MASHED POTATOES AND STEAMED ASPARAGUS. YOU'LL WOW YOUR GUESTS FOR SURE.

## DIRECTIONS

Preheat oven to 375 degrees. In a medium bowl, combine the onion, green bell pepper, eggs, oatmeal, tomato sauce, steak sauce, garlic salt and pepper. Mix with a fork. Add the venison and pork sausage and mix well.

Line an 8x4 inch loaf pan with plastic wrap. Pack the meat mixture into the pan. Invert and unmold the meatloaf onto a lightly oiled baking sheet. Discard the plastic wrap.

Bake until a meat thermometer inserted into the center of the meatloaf reads 160–165 degrees, approximately 1 hour. Remove from oven and let stand for 5 minutes. Cover with foil to keep warm.

In a medium saucepan, melt the butter over medium heat. Add the flour and cook, whisking constantly, until the mixture is lightly browned, approximately 2 minutes. Add the chicken stock and beef bouillon cube and bring to a boil, whisking until thickened and smooth. Reduce heat to medium-low and simmer, whisking often, for 5 minutes. Add the pan juices from the baked meatloaf and milk. Season to taste with salt and pepper. Whisk until heated through.

Slice the meatloaf and serve with a sauceboat of gravy on the side.

# SOUPS, CHILIS AND STEWS

# BLACK BEAN AND VENISON SOUP

## SERVES 4–6

## INGREDIENTS

2 tablespoons butter
2 tablespoons olive oil
1 large onion, chopped
2 carrots, shredded
2 celery stalks, sliced
2 medium green peppers, chopped
1 pound raw ground venison
4 cups beef broth
2 tablespoons tomato paste
16 ounce can stewed tomatoes
1 teaspoon oregano
1 bay leaf
3 cans black beans, drained
red pepper flakes to taste
salt to taste
½ cup sherry (optional)
2 tablespoons lemon juice (optional)
1 tablespoon smoked paprika (optional)

## DIRECTIONS

In a large soup pot or Dutch oven, heat the butter and olive oil over medium heat. Add the onion, carrot, celery and green pepper. Cover and cook until softened. Add the venison and stir together. Cook until the venison is no longer pink.

Stir in the beef broth, tomato paste, stewed tomatoes, oregano and bay leaf. Add the black beans and simmer until all ingredients are heated through. Season to taste with red pepper flakes and salt.

HENRY SAYS: TO GIVE THIS SOUP EXTRA DEPTH OF FLAVOR, ADD ANY OR ALL OF THE OPTIONAL INGREDIENTS WHEN SEASONING WITH THE SALT AND PEPPER.

# CHEESY BEER AND VENISON SOUP

## SERVES 6–8

### INGREDIENTS

¼ cup celery, finely chopped
¼ cup carrot, finely chopped
¼ cup green pepper, finely chopped
¼ cup onion, finely chopped
3 cups chicken broth
2 tablespoons butter
1 pound coarsely ground venison
1 teaspoon salt
¼ teaspoon black pepper
⅓ cup flour
3 cups sharp cheddar cheese, grated
1 12 ounce can beer, room temperature

### DIRECTIONS

Combine celery, carrot, green pepper and onion in a slow cooker. Add the chicken broth, salt and pepper. Cover and cook on low 4 to 5 hours.

Melt the butter in a heavy skillet over medium heat. Add the venison and cook, stirring constantly, until the meat is fully cooked. Add to the broth in the slow cooker.

Turn slow cooker to high. Dissolve flour in ¼ cup of water. Add to the broth, stirring well. Add the cheese, half at a time, stirring until well blended. Pour in beer. Cover and cook on high for 15 to 20 minutes.

## HENRY SAYS: SERVE WITH A CRUSTY BREAD AND A MUG OF, WHAT ELSE, ICE COLD BEER.

# CHUNKY VENISON CHILI

## SERVES 6

## INGREDIENTS

2 tablespoons vegetable oil
2 pounds venison, cut into ¾ inch pieces
2 medium onions, diced
2 15 ounce cans tomato sauce
2 15 ounce cans stewed tomatoes
1 large green pepper, diced
2 tablespoons chili powder
1 teaspoon salt
⅛ teaspoon red pepper
1 teaspoon oregano
1 tablespoon brown sugar
1 tablespoon Cajun seasoning
2 15 ounce cans kidney beans

## DIRECTIONS

In a medium stockpot over medium heat, brown the venison and onions in the vegetable oil. Add the tomato sauce, stewed tomatoes, green pepper, chili powder, salt, red pepper, oregano, brown sugar and Cajun seasoning.

Cover, reduce heat to low and simmer for 2 hours. If not thick, remove the cover for the last 20 minutes. Add the kidney beans just before serving and heat through.

HENRY SAYS: ADD SOME DICED CRAISINS FOR ADDED FLAVOR AND, IF YOU LIKE IT HOT, INCREASE THE RED PEPPER TO ¼ TEASPOON.

# CLASSIC VENISON STEW

SERVES 4–6

## INGREDIENTS

3 pounds venison, cut into 1½ inch pieces
1 teaspoon salt
pepper to taste
3 tablespoons butter
3 cloves garlic, minced
3 medium onions, chopped
2 teaspoons parsley, chopped
2 Leeks, sliced (white part only)
1 bay leaf
2 ounces brandy
1 teaspoon thyme
1 cup chicken stock
2 red wine
3 cans beef broth
2 carrots, sliced
2 packages frozen mixed vegetables

## DIRECTIONS

Season venison with salt and pepper. Melt the butter in a medium Dutch oven and brown the venison.

Stir in the garlic, onions, parsley and leeks. Add the bay leaf and stir to combine.

Add the brandy. Set aflame and stir carefully until the flame is extinguished.

Add the thyme, chicken stock, red wine, beef broth, carrots and mixed vegetables. Bring to a slow boil over medium heat. Reduce heat to low and simmer 2 to 3 hours or until venison is tender. Remove bay leaf and serve.

## HENRY SAYS: THIS DEFINITELY CALLS FOR A BEAR RUG IN FRONT OF A ROARING FIRE.

# CREAMED CORN AND VENISON SOUP

## SERVES 6–8

### INGREDIENTS

2 tablespoons butter
1 scallion, minced
2 teaspoons fresh ginger, minced
2 pounds ground venison
3 17 ounce cans creamed corn
3 cups chicken broth
3 tablespoons teriyaki sauce
1 tablespoon dry sherry
1 tablespoon cornstarch

### DIRECTIONS

In a large saucepan or Dutch oven melt the butter over medium-high heat. Add the scallion and ginger, and stir-fry until fragrant, approximately 30 seconds. Add the venison and stir-fry until no longer pink, approximately 3 minutes.

Stir in the creamed corn, chicken broth, teriyaki sauce and dry sherry. Reduce heat to low and simmer for 20 minutes.

In a small bowl, mix the cornstarch with 2 tablespoons water. Add the cornstarch mixture to the simmering soup and cook, stirring occasionally, until thickened, about 3 minutes.

## HENRY SAYS: GRAB A FRENCH BAGUETTE AT YOUR FAVORITE BAKERY AND KICK BACK WITH A BOWL OF SOUP AND TOASTED BREAD ROUNDS—THE PERFECT WAY TO SPEND A CHILLY WEEKEND AFTERNOON.

# CREAMY TOMATO SOUP WITH VENISON DUMPLINGS

## INGREDIENTS

3 8 ounce cans creamy tomato with bacon and cheese soup
1 15 ounce can stewed tomatoes, chopped
1 pound ground venison
1 pound bulk sweet Italian sausage
1 egg, beaten
½ cup Italian seasoned bread crumbs

## DIRECTIONS

In a large Dutch oven, combine the tomato soup and stewed tomatoes, and bring to a simmer over medium heat.

In a large bowl, combine the venison, sausage, egg and bread crumbs, mixing well. Form into approximately 30 balls and add to the simmering soup. Cook about 15 minutes or until the dumplings are cooked through. Serve with dark rye bread.

HENRY SAYS: THIS IS A GREAT WAY TO CREATE A SUBSTANTIAL MEAL WITH PANTRY INGREDIENTS.

# FARMHOUSE VENISON

## SERVES 6–8

## INGREDIENTS

2 pounds venison, cut into 1 inch cubes
1 teaspoon seasoned salt
½ teaspoon white pepper
1 teaspoon paprika
1 cup ketchup
2 medium zucchini, cut into 1 inch slices
2 medium yellow squash, cut into 1 inch slices
2 cups chicken stock
1 15 ounce can whole kernel corn
2 tablespoons cornstarch
3 tablespoons water

## DIRECTIONS

Season the venison with the salt, pepper and paprika. Place in a slow cooker with the chicken stock and ketchup. Cover and cook on low 6 to 8 hours, or until venison is fork tender. Increase heat to high, stir in corn, zucchini and yellow squash. Dissolve the cornstarch in the water and stir into the meat mixture in the slow cooker. Continue cooking for 10 to 20 minutes until thickened.

HENRY SAYS: THIS IS A GREAT MEAL TO MAKE A DAY OR TWO AHEAD. JUST REHEAT IN THE MICROWAVE AND SERVE OVER WIDE EGG NOODLES.

# ITALIAN VENISON MEATBALL STEW

## SERVES 6–8

## INGREDIENTS

2 carrots, chopped ½ inch thick
½ cup seasoned bread crumbs
½ cup Parmesan cheese, shredded
2 eggs, beaten
¼ cup milk
1 teaspoon celery salt
¼ teaspoon granulated garlic
¼ teaspoon white pepper
2 pounds ground venison
1 teaspoon Italian seasoning
8 sweet Italian sausages
1 cup beef bouillon
2 15 ounce cans stewed tomatoes, chopped
1 package Italian-style vegetables

## DIRECTIONS

Arrange the carrots to cover the bottom of a slow cooker.

In a large bowl, combine the bread crumbs, cheese, eggs, milk, celery salt, granulated garlic and pepper. Mix in the venison and combine well. Form into 2 inch meatballs and place on the carrots.

Sprinkle with the Italian seasoning and add the sausage. Pour in the bouillon and tomatoes and cook on low 5 to 6 hours. Turn heat to high, add the vegetables and cook 15 to 20 minutes.

HENRY SAYS: SERVE WITH ANY SMALL PASTA LIKE ROTINI, DITALINI, FARFALLE OR SHELLS.

# SLOW COOKER VENISON STEW

## SERVES 4–6

## INGREDIENTS

2 pounds venison, cut into 1 inch pieces
2 medium onions, chopped
2 stalks celery, sliced
3 medium red potatoes, cut into 1 inch cubes
6 carrots, sliced ¾ inch thick
1 slice white bread, cubed
1 15 ounce can stewed tomatoes
1 tablespoon brown sugar
1 tablespoon teriyaki sauce
1 teaspoon salt
4 teaspoon pepper
1 cup water
½ cup dried apples, chopped
½ cup craisins

## DIRECTIONS

Place all ingredients in a slow cooker set on low. Cook 8 to 10 hours.

## HENRY SAYS: HOW EASY IS THIS? FOR A MORE ROBUST FLAVOR, REPLACE THE WATER WITH A DRY RED WINE.

# SPLIT PEA AND LENTIL SOUP WITH VENISON AND BACON DUMPLINGS

## SERVES 4–6

### INGREDIENTS

½ pound dried split peas
½ pound lentils
4 tablespoons butter
1 medium onion, finely chopped
2 carrots, finely chopped
2 stalks celery, finely chopped
8 cups chicken stock
2 medium Yukon gold potatoes, shredded
1 teaspoon sea salt
¼ teaspoon white pepper
2 tablespoons Italian salad dressing
6 strips pre-cooked bacon, shredded
1 bay leaf
1 pound ground venison
4 strips pre-cooked bacon, shredded
1 egg
¼ teaspoon seasoned salt
¼ teaspoon white pepper

**HENRY SAYS: THICK AND RICH WITH JUST A HINT OF SMOKE FROM THE BACON.**

### DIRECTIONS

In a large saucepan, combine the split peas and lentils. Add 1 quart water and bring to a boil over high heat. Cook for 3 minutes. Remove the saucepan from the heat, cover and let stand for 1 hour. Drain, reserving the liquid.

In a large Dutch oven, melt the butter. Add the onion, carrots and celery and sauté until tender.

Add the split pea and lentil mixture, reserved liquid, chicken stock, potatoes, salt, pepper, salad dressing and 6 strips of shredded bacon. Bring to a boil over medium heat. Add the bay leaf, reduce heat to low and simmer until the split peas and lentils are tender, about 40 minutes.

In a medium bowl, combine the ground venison, 4 strips shredded bacon, egg, salt and pepper. Form into ¾ inch dumplings and add to the simmering soup. Simmer for 15 to 20 minutes, or until dumplings are cooked through.

# VENISON AND NOODLE SOUP

## SERVES 4–6

### INGREDIENTS

4 cups chicken stock
4 tablespoons ground raw venison
2 packages Ramen Noodles (discard the seasoning packet)
¼ teaspoon white pepper
1 cup raw bean sprouts
3 cloves garlic, finely minced
2 tablespoons teriyaki sauce
2 tablespoons fish sauce
2 tablespoons oyster sauce
2 large lettuce leaves, shredded
1 tablespoon fresh coriander leaves, shredded
½ teaspoon sriracha sauce
1 tablespoon brown sugar
½ pound cooked venison roast, thinly sliced

### DIRECTIONS

In a large saucepan, heat the chicken stock over medium heat. Add the ground venison and simmer for 3 to 4 minutes, stirring to break up the venison.

Break the Ramen Noodles into 4 sections each. Add to the stock and simmer until tender (6 to 8 minutes).

Stir in the pepper, bean sprouts, garlic, teriyaki sauce, fish sauce, oyster sauce, lettuce, coriander, sriracha sauce and brown sugar. Simmer for 3 to 5 minutes.

Add the cooked venison and simmer until heated through.

## HENRY SAYS: BE SURE TO KEEP SOME ON HAND FOR THOSE WINTER COLDS.

# VENISON AND ORZO STEW

## SERVES 6–8

## INGREDIENTS

2½ pounds venison, cut into 2 inch cubes
1 quart water
2 cups red wine
2 large onions, sliced
3 large carrots, cut into 1 inch pieces
2 15 ounce cans stewed tomatoes, chopped
1 teaspoon seasoned salt
¼ teaspoon black pepper
1 tablespoon smoked paprika
1 cup orzo pasta cooked in 4 cups chicken stock

## DIRECTIONS

Place all ingredients except the pasta in a slow cooker. Cover and cook on low for 4 to 5 hours. Adjust seasoning with additional salt and pepper. Stir in cooked pasta and heat for 20 more minutes.

HENRY SAYS: TRY A MIXED GREEN SALAD WITH GARLIC CROUTONS, A LIGHT VINAIGRETTE AND SOME REALLY BOLD SHAVED CHEESE WITH THIS STEW.

# VENISON AND POTATO CHOWDER

## SERVES 6–8

## INGREDIENTS
2 tablespoons butter
1 pound ground venison
6 strips pre-cooked bacon, chopped
1 medium white onion, chopped
2 stalks celery, sliced
1 large red bell pepper, diced
8 cups chicken stock
2 medium Yukon gold potatoes, cut into ½ inch cubes
1 bay leaf
1 teaspoon marjoram
½ teaspoon salt
¼ teaspoon white pepper
1 cup heavy cream

## DIRECTIONS
In a large saucepan or Dutch oven, melt the butter over medium heat and cook the venison, bacon, onion, celery and red pepper for 5 to 8 minutes, stirring occasionally.

Add the chicken stock, potato, bay leaf, marjoram, salt and white pepper.
Bring to a boil and reduce heat to low.

Simmer, stirring occasionally, until potatoes are tender. Stir in heavy cream and heat through.

## HENRY SAYS: A MEAL IN A BOWL.

# VENISON BARLEY SOUP

## SERVES 4–6

## INGREDIENTS

2 tablespoons butter
1 pound coarsely ground venison
1 15 ounce can tomato paste
½ cup quick cooking barley
2 15 ounce cans chicken broth
2 tablespoons Worcestershire sauce
3 tablespoons steak sauce
1 tablespoons brown sugar
2 packages frozen mixed vegetables

## DIRECTIONS

In a 4-quart stockpot, melt the butter over medium heat and brown the venison. Stir in the tomato paste, barley and chicken broth. Heat to boiling, stirring occasionally. Add the Worcestershire sauce, steak sauce and brown sugar and stir well. Add the vegetables, reduce heat to low and simmer, covered, for 10 to 15 minutes or until barley is tender.

## HENRY SAYS: IF BARLEY ISN'T ONE OF YOUR FAVORITE GRAINS, SUBSTITUTE WITH FINE NOODLES OR COOKED RICE.

# VENISON HUNGARIAN GOULASH

## SERVES 6–8

## INGREDIENTS

3 pounds venison shoulder, cut into 1½ inch cubes
½ cup flour, seasoned with ¼ teaspoon salt and ¼ teaspoon white pepper
¼ cup butter
2 tablespoons olive oil
3 medium onions, thickly sliced, then cut in half
3 large green peppers, seed and cut into 1x2 inch strips
2 cloves garlic, minced
3 carrots, thinly sliced
2 stalks celery, thickly sliced
2 tablespoons sweet Hungarian paprika
2 15 ounce cans stewed tomatoes, chopped
2 cups chicken stock
1 can tomato paste
1 cup sour cream

## DIRECTIONS

Dredge the venison in the seasoned flour. In a large skillet, heat the butter and olive oil over medium heat. Brown the venison on all sides in several batches. Transfer each batch to a slow cooker.

Add the onions, green peppers, garlic, carrots and celery to the skillet. Stir and sauté for 7 to 10 minutes. Add the paprika and tomatoes, and stir in the tomato paste. Simmer for 10 minutes.

Pour the vegetable and tomato mixture over the venison in the slow cooker. Cover and cook on low 5 hours. Check meat for tenderness and adjust seasoning. Cook an additional hour if required. Add the sour cream and serve with buttered egg noodles.

## HENRY SAYS: GOULASH IS ALSO A POPULAR MEAL IN CENTRAL AND SOUTHERN EUROPE AND SCANDINAVIA.

# VENISON IRISH STEW

## SERVES 4–6

## INGREDIENTS

3 pounds venison, cut into 1½ inch cubes
4 stalks celery, sliced into 1 inch pieces
3 12 ounce cans V-8 Juice
1 tablespoon brown sugar
1 tablespoon quick-cooking tapioca
3 medium onions, quartered then cut in half
6 carrots, sliced into 1 inch pieces
½ teaspoon dried basil
4 potatoes, peeled and cut into 1½ inch pieces

## DIRECTIONS

Preheat oven to 300 degrees.

Combine the venison, onions, celery and carrots in a 2½ quart casserole. Combine the V-8 Juice, tapioca, sugar, salt, pepper and basil in a medium bowl. Pour over the meat and vegetables.

Cover and bake for 2½ hours. Add the potatoes and bake 1 hour longer.

## HENRY SAYS: IRISH SODA BREAD AND AN IRISH STOUT WILL MAKE THIS DISH A MEAL.

# VENISON MINESTRONE SOUP

## SERVES 6–8

## INGREDIENTS

1½ pounds ground venison
3 cups chicken stock
3 cups white wine
1 medium onion, chopped
1 teaspoon garlic salt
1 teaspoon thyme
¼ teaspoon white pepper
2 tablespoons parsley, minced
2 15 ounce cans stewed tomatoes, chopped
1 medium zucchini, thinly sliced
1 15 ounce can garbanzo beans
1 package cabbage cole slaw mix
1 cup small elbow macaroni
½ cup Parmesan cheese, grated

## DIRECTIONS

In a slow cooker, combine the venison with the chicken stock, wine, onion, garlic salt, thyme, pepper, parsley and tomatoes, making sure to break up the venison. Cover and cook on low 6 to 8 hours.

Turn to high and add the zucchini, garbanzo beans, cabbage and macaroni. Cover and cook an additional 30 to 40 minutes, or until the pasta is tender. Place in serving bowls and dust each portion with Parmesan cheese.

## HENRY SAYS: MAKE SURE TO HAVE ENOUGH WHITE WINE ON HAND TO SERVE WITH THE SOUP.

# VENISON RAGOUT

## SERVES 6–8

## INGREDIENTS
3 tablespoons olive oil
3 pounds venison, cut into 1 inch pieces
¼ pound fresh button mushrooms
2 dozen pearl onions, peeled
½ cup beef stock
1 can tomato paste
1½ cups red wine
¾ cup dry sherry
¼ cup ruby port
4 tablespoons flour
1 clove garlic, crushed
¼ teaspoon black pepper
2 bay leaves

## DIRECTIONS
Preheat oven to 350 degrees.

Heat the olive oil in a Dutch oven over medium heat and brown the venison in batches, if necessary. Transfer the venison to bowl. Add the mushrooms and onions to the Dutch oven and cook, stirring constantly, until the onions begin to brown. Turn the heat off and remove the onions and mushrooms to the bowl with the venison. Add the beef stock and tomato paste to the Dutch oven and mix well.

In a separate bowl, combine the red wine, sherry and port with the flour to form a thin paste. Add this mixture to the Dutch oven and increase the heat to medium, stirring constantly until the mixture almost boils. Add the venison, mushrooms, onions, garlic, pepper and bay leaves. Cover and bake for 1½ to 2 hours, or until the venison is tender. Serve over buttered noodles.

## HENRY SAYS: THE TERM RAGOUT COMES FROM THE FRENCH RAGOÛTER, MEANING: "TO REVIVE THE TASTE."

# VENISON SPEAKEASY STEW

## SERVES 6–8

## INGREDIENTS

3 pounds venison, cut into 2 inch pieces
½ cup flour, mixed with ¼ teaspoon garlic salt and ¼ teaspoon pepper
¼ cup olive oil
3 large onions, sliced and chopped
6 cloves garlic, minced
½ pound thick-cut bacon, chopped
1½ teaspoons curry powder
1 can cream of celery soup
1 can tomato soup
12 ounces beer
3 cups water
¼ cup bourbon

## DIRECTIONS

Dredge the venison in the seasoned flour.

In a large Dutch oven, heat the olive oil over medium heat. Add the venison and brown on all sides. Stir in the onion, garlic, bacon and curry powder. Reduce heat to low and sauté, stirring constantly for 10 minutes.

In a large bowl, mix together the soups, beer, water and bourbon. Pour over the venison and mix well. Cover and simmer over low heat for 1 hour, or until venison is fork tender.

## HENRY SAYS: THIS STEW CAN BE SERVED OVER RICE, STEAMED POTATOES OR TOASTED BREAD. AND, OF COURSE, IT ALWAYS NEEDS A PINT NEARBY.

# VENISON VEGETABLE SOUP

## SERVES 4–6

## INGREDIENTS

2 tablespoons butter
½ pound ground venison
1 small onion, sliced and chopped
¼ teaspoon salt
3 cups chicken stock
1 46 ounce can tomato juice
1 10 ounce package frozen mixed vegetables
½ cup orzo pasta
¼ teaspoon black pepper

## DIRECTIONS

Melt the butter in a 4-quart saucepan. Add the venison, onion and salt and cook over medium heat until the venison is browned. Add the chicken stock, tomato juice and vegetables. Bring to a boil. Add the pasta and pepper. Reduce heat and simmer for 10 minutes, or until pasta is tender.

## HENRY SAYS: TRY SERVING THIS IN A BREAD BOWL.

# SANDWICHES

# BOILED VENISON

## INGREDIENTS
3 pounds boneless venison shoulder or leg roast
2 large onions, sliced
3 large carrots, sliced
1 teaspoon seasoned salt
3 cups chicken stock

## DIRECTIONS
Place the roast in the bottom of a large Dutch oven. Add the onions, carrots, salt and chicken stock. Cover and simmer over low heat for 3 hours. The meat should be tender but not stringy.

Remove from the heat and allow the meat to cool in the broth. Move the meat to a non-stick pan and cover with plastic wrap. Refrigerate until ready to use.

## HENRY SAYS: SLICE AND USE BOILED VENISON FOR COLD OR HOT SANDWICHES (MAKES A GREAT RUEBEN).

# DONNIE'S VENISON BURGER

## SERVES 4

## INGREDIENTS

3 tablespoons butter
2 medium onions, sliced
1 green pepper, cut into strips
1 cup fresh mushrooms
dash sherry
1½ pounds ground venison
4 slices cheddar cheese
1 teaspoon Kitchen Bouquet
¼ cup barbecue sauce
½ teaspoon Worcestershire sauce

## DIRECTIONS

In a large skillet over medium heat, melt 2 tablespoons butter and sauté the onion, green pepper and mushrooms until golden brown. Add the sherry and transfer this mixture to a bowl.

Form the venison into 4 thick patties. Melt the remaining tablespoon of butter in the skillet and cook the patties over medium heat until browned on both sides. Transfer to a plate and top each with a slice of cheese.

Add ¼ cup water to skillet drippings and stir. Add Kitchen Bouquet, barbecue sauce, Worcestershire sauce and the vegetables. Stir and simmer over medium heat for 5 minutes.

Return burgers to the skillet. Cover and simmer until the cheese begins to melt, about 5 minutes. Serve open-faced on a whole-grain bun with a healthy portion of the sauce on top.

## HENRY SAYS: A VINEGAR-BASED POTATO SALAD OR COLESLAW WILL ROUND OUT THIS MEAL PERFECTLY.

# HOT DOG VENISON CHILI SAUCE

## INGREDIENTS
1 pound ground venison
1 teaspoon cumin
1 cup chicken stock
1½ teaspoons chili powder
½ teaspoon garlic powder
1 tablespoon brown sugar
¼ cup ketchup
1 teaspoon dried onion flakes
dash of salt
2 tablespoons yellow mustard

## DIRECTIONS
Combine all ingredients in a medium saucepan. Cook over low heat for 10 to 15 minutes, or until thickened. Stir occasionally to break up the venison and distribute the seasonings.

## HENRY SAYS: YOUR FRIENDS WON'T EAT A PLAIN HOT DOG EVER AGAIN. TRY ADDING ONION SLICES ON TOP—YUM.

# MAC'S LOOSE MEAT VENISON SANDWICH

SERVES 4–6

## INGREDIENTS

1 pound ground venison
½ pound bulk mild Italian sausage
1 small onion, minced
1 16 ounce can baked beans
1 cup pepper jack cheese, shredded

## DIRECTIONS

In a large skillet, sauté the venison, sausage and onion over medium heat until cooked through. Stir in the beans and cheese, and cook until the cheese has melted. Serve on an egg bun.

HENRY SAYS: AND IOWA THOUGHT THEY HAD
A LOCK ON THE LOOSE MEAT SANDWICH.

# SPANISH VENISON BURGERS

## SERVES 8

## INGREDIENTS

1 pound ground venison
½ pound chorizo sausage
½ pound pork sausage
¼ cup green olives, pitted and chopped
1 large egg, beaten
½ cup pine nuts
1 teaspoon garlic salt
½ teaspoon nutmeg
¼ teaspoon white pepper
2 teaspoons smoked paprika
¼ cup craisins, soaked in ⅓ cup port wine

## DIRECTIONS

Place all ingredients in a large bowl and mix well. Divide into 8 equal portions and form into thick patties. Cook on the grill or in a skillet on the stove over medium high heat until desired degree of doneness is achieved.

## HENRY SAYS: CRUMBLE BLEU CHEESE ON TOP FOR THE LAST SEVERAL MINUTES OF COOKING TO ADD AN EXTRA DIMENSION OF FLAVOR.

# SPICY VENISON BURGERS

## SERVES 6–8

## INGREDIENTS

1½ pounds ground venison
½ pound bulk hot Italian sausage
1 egg, beaten
⅓ cup seasoned bread crumbs
2 tablespoons butter
2 tablespoons olive oil
1 small onion, sliced and chopped
1 small green pepper, sliced and chopped
2 stalks celery, sliced
1 15 ounce can stewed tomatoes, chopped
¼ teaspoon granulated garlic
¼ cup Worcestershire sauce
¼ cup green olives, pitted and sliced
1 cup red wine

## DIRECTIONS

Preheat oven to 325 degrees. In a large bowl, combine the venison, sausage, egg and bread crumbs. Divide into 8 portions and form thick patties.

In a heavy skillet, melt the butter and brown the patties on both sides. Transfer to a buttered baking dish.

Add the olive oil to the skillet and sauté the onion, green pepper and celery over low heat for 5 minutes. Add the remaining ingredients. Bring to a boil. Pour over the patties, cover and bake 1 hour and 20 minutes. Serve on your favorite bun or bread and don't forget a generous portion of the sauce.

## HENRY SAYS: INCREASE THE HEAT WITH HOT SAUCE OR RED PEPPER FLAKES.

# STUFFED BURGERS

## SERVES 6

### INGREDIENTS

2 slices bread, soaked in ½ cup milk
1½ pounds ground venison
1½ pounds ground pork or pork sausage
2 eggs, beaten
¼ teaspoon smoked paprika
1 tablespoon Worcestershire sauce
3 ounces bleu or Stilton cheese
3 ounces cream cheese
1 tablespoon capers, minced
6 strips thick-cut bacon
freshly ground pepper to taste

### DIRECTIONS

Squeeze the milk from the bread. In a food processor, combine the bread with the pork and venison. Pulse chop to combine. Transfer to a large bowl. Mix in the beaten egg, paprika and Worcestershire sauce. Divide into 6 balls, cut each in half and form into 3 inch diameter patties. Cover and refrigerate.

In a medium bowl, mix together the cheeses, capers and pepper. Transfer to a sheet of plastic wrap. Form into a cylinder 6 inch long. Wrap in the plastic wrap and put into freezer for at least 1 hour. Remove from freezer and cut into 6 equal portions.

Place a piece of the cheese mixture on a venison patty, top with a second patty. Form the venison so it completely covers the cheese. Wrap the patty with a strip of bacon. Fasten with a round toothpick. Season with pepper.

Heat a large heavy skillet over medium high heat. Melt 2 tablespoons butter. Add the burgers and brown on each side. Transfer to a baking dish. Bake in a 325 degree oven for 15 minutes.

## HENRY SAYS: THESE BURGERS CAN BE CASUALLY SERVED ON A BUN OR ELEGANTLY SERVED WITH SAUCE BÉARNAISE.

# VENISON SLOPPY JOES

## SERVES 6–8

### INGREDIENTS

3 tablespoons butter
2 pounds ground venison
1 pound ground beef
1 large onion, finely chopped
2 carrots, grated
1 teaspoon garlic, chopped
1 can vegetable soup
1 12 ounce can V-8 Juice
1 teaspoon brown sugar

### DIRECTIONS

In a large sauté pan over medium heat, melt the butter. Add the venison and beef and cook, stirring constantly, until brown. Stir in the onions, carrots and garlic and sauté until the onions are soft. Mix in the soup, juice and brown sugar. Heat thoroughly.

## HENRY SAYS: SERVE ON FRESHLY BAKED EGG BUNS WITH DILL PICKLE CHIPS AND SEASONED SWEET POTATO FRIES.

# SAUSAGE

# CHEESE AND BACON MEETS VENISON

## SERVES 8

## INGREDIENTS

1½ pounds ground venison
8 strips pre-cooked bacon
6 ounces white cheddar cheese
1 cup cheese crackers, crumbled in a food processor
2 green onions, thinly sliced
3 tablespoons ketchup
2 eggs, beaten
½ teaspoon granulated garlic
¼ teaspoon white pepper
1 small can sliced black olives

## DIRECTIONS

In a large bowl, mix together the venison, bacon, cheese, crackers and onions. Add the ketchup, eggs, granulated garlic, pepper and olives. Mix well. Divide into 8 equal portions and form into sausage links. Place on a non-stick baking tray. Bake for 20 minutes or until thermometer inserted in center reaches 160 degrees. Serve on hoagie buns with your choice of condiments.

## HENRY SAYS: USING DIFFERENT CHEESES SIGNIFICANTLY CHANGES THE FLAVOR OF THESE SAUSAGES—TRY PEPPER JACK TO ADD A LITTLE SPICE.

# VENISON BRATWURST

## 32 BRATWURST

## INGREDIENTS

4 pounds venison, coarsely ground
4 pounds pork shoulder or pork butt, coarsely ground
8 ounces German ale
3 tablespoons Morton's Tender Quick
3 tablespoons Penzey's Bratwurst Seasoning
2 teaspoons ground coriander
2 teaspoons white sugar

## DIRECTIONS

In a large bowl, combine all ingredients and mix well. Cover and refrigerate for 24 hours. Mix again and stuff natural casing forming links about 6 inches long. Remove any air pockets by piercing with a large needle.

Package in plastic bags, separating sausages with wax paper, and freeze for later use.

To prepare the sausage, defrost. Place in a deep skillet over high heat with 1 cup water. Bring to a boil, cover, reduce heat to low and simmer for 10 minutes. Pour off any remaining water. Add one tablespoon of oil, increase heat to medium-high and cook until sausages are browned.

HENRY SAYS: YOU CAN ALSO FOREGO THE CASINGS AND FORM THE MEAT MIXTURE INTO PATTIES FOR COOKING ON THE GRILL AND SERVING ON RYE OR PRETZEL BUNS.

# VENISON BREAKFAST SAUSAGE

## 8 PATTIES

### INGREDIENTS

1 pound ground venison
½ pound ground pork
1 tablespoon Penzey's Bavarian-Style Seasoning
2 tablespoons water

### DIRECTIONS

In a medium bowl, thoroughly mix all ingredients. Form into patties about ¼ inch thick.

Heat 1 tablespoon vegetable oil in a heavy skillet over medium heat. Fry the patties until they are cooked through and browned on both sides.

## HENRY SAYS: THESE PATTIES FREEZE WELL. YOU CAN ALSO MAKE A LARGER QUANTITY AND FORM INTO SAUSAGE LINKS USING NATURAL CASINGS.

# VENISON CHORIZO SAUSAGE

## INGREDIENTS

2 pounds ground venison
2 pounds slab bacon, coarsely ground
2 tablespoons smoked paprika
1 tablespoon celery salt
½ teaspoon black pepper
½ teaspoon white pepper
2 teaspoons red pepper, crushed
2 teaspoons brown sugar
1 teaspoon granulated garlic
½ teaspoon oregano, crushed
½ teaspoon cumin, ground
¼ cup red wine vinegar

## DIRECTIONS

In a large bowl, combine the venison and bacon.

Combine the remaining ingredients in a small bowl. Add this mixture to the meats and mix well. Cover and refrigerate 2 hours.

Divide into 8 ounce portions and freeze.

To use, thaw and cook over medium heat, stirring occasionally until browned and cooked through.

## HENRY SAYS: USE CHORIZO IN SCRAMBLED EGGS, OMELETTES, TACOS, CHILI, STEWS OR ANY DISH THAT NEEDS SOME "SPARKLE."

# VENISON SALAMI

## 3 2 POUND SAUSAGES

## INGREDIENTS

5 pounds venison, coarsely ground
2 pounds pork shoulder, coarsely ground
1½ tablespoons pepper, coarsely ground
2½ teaspoons garlic powder
1½ teaspoons barbecue seasoning
5 teaspoons Morton's Tender Quick
1½ teaspoon hickory smoked salt
1½ teaspoon onion flakes

## DIRECTIONS

In a large stainless steel bowl, combine all ingredients. Mix well, cover and refrigerate at least 24 hours. Repeat the mixing and refrigeration process each day for 3 days.

Preheat oven to 150 degrees. Shape the meat mixture into 3 logs. Place on an oiled rack in a shallow baking pan and bake 6 to 7 hours. Remove excess cooking juices as necessary. Remove from oven, cool the salami, wrap in plastic wrap and store in the refrigerator.

## HENRY SAYS: ADD EXTRA FLAVOR BY SMOKING FOR ABOUT AN HOUR. THE SALAMI CAN BE FROZEN.

# VENISON SAUSAGE SLIDERS

## INGREDIENTS

2 pounds ground venison
1 pound fatty pork
2 medium onions, ground
1 tablespoon garlic, chopped
3 tablespoons fresh parsley, chopped
1 tablespoons seasoned salt
½ tablespoon ground cumin
½ tablespoon ground nutmeg

## DIRECTIONS

In a large bowl, combine all ingredients and mix thoroughly. Form into 1½ inch balls, place on tray and freeze for 3 hours. Remove from the freezer and package for freezer storage.

To prepare, defrost. Preheat a heavy skillet over medium heat. Add the sausage balls and flatten with a fork. Cook until brown, about 3 minutes. Turn and cook another 3 minutes.

## HENRY SAYS: IF YOU LIKE YOUR SAUSAGE SPICY, ADD HOT SAUCE TO TASTE. SERVE ON A SMALL BUN WITH YOUR FAVORITE CONDIMENTS.

# VENISON SUMMER SAUSAGE

## INGREDIENTS

2 pounds ground venison
1 pound slab bacon, coarsely ground
1 teaspoon granulated garlic
½ teaspoon onion powder
2 teaspoons Morton's Tender Quick
2 teaspoons Liquid Smoke
¼ teaspoon cracked pepper
¼ teaspoon white pepper
½ teaspoon mustard seed
1 cup ice water

## DIRECTIONS

In a large bowl, combine all the ingredients.

Form into 2 rolls. Wrap in heavy duty foil (shiny side toward the meat). Refrigerate for 24 hours.

Preheat oven to 300 degrees. Place the rolls on a pan fitted with a rack. Poke holes in the foil on the bottom of the rolls to allow the liquid to drain. Bake 2 hours. Remove from oven, unwrap and cool completely before slicing.

## HENRY SAYS: MAKES A GREAT APPETIZER SERVED WITH CHEESE, CRACKERS AND GRAPES. ANY UNUSED PORTIONS CAN BE FROZEN.

# VENISON, POTATO AND SAUERKRAUT SAUSAGE

## 6 SAUSAGES

## INGREDIENTS

1 pound venison, cut into 1 inch cubes
1 pound pork shoulder, cut into 1 inch cubes
6 strips pre-cooked bacon, cut into ½ inch pieces
½ pound Yukon gold potatoes, cooked, peeled and cut in 1 inch pieces
1 cup sauerkraut, drained, rinsed and dried on paper towels

## SPICE BLEND

¼ teaspoon white pepper
¼ teaspoon dry-rubbed sage
¼ teaspoon dry-rubbed basil
1 teaspoon salt
2 tablespoons brown sugar
½ teaspoon smoked paprika
1 large egg, beaten

## DIRECTIONS

In a large bowl, combine the venison, pork, bacon, potatoes and sauerkraut. In a small bowl, combine the spice blend ingredients and mix well. Add the spice blend to the meats and mix well. Cover and refrigerate at least 1 hour.

Remove sausage mixture from the refrigerator. Grind or chop mixture to a uniform consistency. Add the egg and use your hands to thoroughly mix.

Divide the mixture into 8 ounce portions. Roll into balls and flatten between two sheets of wax paper. Using a non-stick skillet over medium heat, melt 1 tablespoon butter and 2 tablespoons olive oil. Brown the sausage patties 3 to 4 minutes on each side or until cooked through.

## HENRY SAYS: I PREFER A PRETTY COARSE GRIND ON THIS SAUSAGE AND MY FAVORITE PRESENTATION IS ON A KAISER BUN WITH DIJON MUSTARD.

# ROASTS, STEAKS AND CHOPS

# APPLE CIDER VENISON POT ROAST

## SERVES 6–8

## INGREDIENTS

3½ to 4 pound venison roast
2 onions, sliced
6 whole cloves
1 piece ginger root
1 small piece cinnamon stick
1½ teaspoons salt
2 cups apple cider
2 tablespoons butter

## DIRECTIONS

Mix the onion, cloves, ginger root, cinnamon stick, salt and cider in a large bowl. Add the venison. Cover and refrigerate overnight.

Melt the butter in a large Dutch oven. Remove the venison from the marinade and brown slowly over medium heat in the Dutch oven. Add the marinade, cover and simmer over low heat for about 2½ hours or until meat is cooked through. Serve with pan juices which you can thicken if you like.

## HENRY SAYS: IF YOU PREFER, AFTER BROWNING THE ROAST, YOU CAN COMPLETE THE COOKING IN A SLOW COOKER FOR 4 TO 5 HOURS ON LOW.

# BAKED VENISON CHOPS

## SERVES 4

## INGREDIENTS

4 thick venison chops
1 teaspoon seasoned salt
1 teaspoon white pepper
1 large onion, sliced
2 stalks celery, sliced
1 15 ounce can stewed tomatoes, chopped
1 cup white wine

## DIRECTIONS

Preheat oven to 325 degrees. Season the chops with the seasoned salt and pepper. Arrange in a single layer in a baking pan. Cover with the sliced onion and celery and top with the stewed tomatoes. Pour the wine on top and bake 40 to 45 minutes. At 20 minutes, turn the chops over.

## HENRY SAYS: SERVE WITH THE TOMATOES, ONION AND CELERY ON A BED OF RICE.

# BARBECUED VENISON CHOPS

## SERVES 4–6

## INGREDIENTS
8 venison chops
½ cup olive oil
1 teaspoon Madras curry powder
1 tablespoon onion, minced
1 teaspoon garlic, minced
½ cup red wine vinegar
½ cup honey
½ cup spicy barbecue sauce

## DIRECTIONS
Arrange chops on tray.

In a medium saucepan, combine remaining ingredients over low heat and simmer for 15 minutes.

Brush chops with sauce on both sides. Grill over medium heat for 3 minutes. Do a quarter turn and grill an additional 3 minutes. Flip chops to the other side, baste with sauce and repeat the first two steps. You now have perfectly marked medium-rare to medium venison chops. Serve a bowl of the sauce on the side.

## HENRY SAYS: WATCH THE CHOPS CLOSELY ON THE GRILL. THE SAUCE HAS A HIGH SUGAR CONTENT AND CAN BURN EASILY.

# BRAISED VENISON WITH APPLES AND CRAISINS

## SERVES 6–8

## INGREDIENTS

½ cup brown sugar
¼ cup teriyaki sauce
1 cup chicken stock
2 large apples, peeled, cored and sliced ¼ inch thick
2 medium onions, finely chopped
¼ cup craisins, soaked in ½ cup red wine or whiskey for 10 minutes
4 pounds boneless venison, cut in serving pieces

## DIRECTIONS

In a slow cooker, mix together the brown sugar, teriyaki sauce and chicken stock. Layer the apples with the onions and craisins (including liquid) in the slow cooker. Add the venison on top and baste with the liquid.

Cover and cook on low 4 to 5 hours, basting the venison occasionally.

## HENRY SAYS: SERVE WITH BROWN RICE AND YOUR CHOICE OF VEGETABLE.

# CHICKEN-FRIED VENISON STEAK

## SERVES 6–8

## INGREDIENTS

2 pounds boneless venison steak, sliced ½ inch thick
1 cup flour, seasoned with ½ teaspoon salt, ¼ teaspoon white pepper and 2 teaspoons paprika
3 tablespoons olive oil
2 medium onions, sliced
1 cup mushrooms, sliced
1 15 ounce can tomato paste, mixed with 1 teaspoon sugar
1 cup heavy cream

## DIRECTIONS

Preheat oven to 300 degrees.

Dredge the venison in the seasoned flour. In a heavy skillet, heat the olive oil over medium heat and brown the venison on both sides. Transfer the venison to a buttered oven-proof dish. Add the onions and mushrooms.

Mix together the tomato paste and cream. Season to taste with salt and pepper and pour over the venison and vegetables. Bake for 2 hours or until venison is tender.

### HENRY SAYS: YOU CAN COOK THE STEAKS IN THE SKILLET ON TOP OF THE STOVE OVER LOW HEAT. JUST COVER THE SKILLET AND CHECK THE LIQUID LEVEL OFTEN.

# CUBAN PULLED VENISON

## SERVES 6–8

### INGREDIENTS

2 tablespoons olive oil
2 large green peppers, seeded and coarsely chopped
2 medium onions, sliced and coarsely chopped
3 cloves garlic, chopped
1 tablespoon cumin, ground
1 tablespoon oregano
2 cups chicken stock
1 15 ounce can stewed tomatoes, chopped
4 pounds boneless venison, large pieces
4 spicy chorizo sausages
1 cup pimento-stuffed olives, sliced
1 tablespoon red wine vinegar
8 cups white rice, cooked

### DIRECTIONS

Preheat oven to 325 degrees.

In a large heavy Dutch oven, heat the olive oil over medium heat. Sauté the peppers, onions and garlic for 8 to 10 minutes. Stir in the cumin, oregano, chicken stock and tomatoes. Heat to a simmer and add the venison and sausages. Cover and place in the oven. Bake for 3 to 4 hours or until the venison is tender.

Transfer the venison and sausage to separate bowls. Shred the venison and return to the Dutch oven. Thinly slice the sausage and return to the Dutch oven. Stir in the olives and vinegar. Serve in bowls over white rice.

## HENRY SAYS: GARNISH EACH SERVING WITH SLICED GREEN ONIONS AND FRESH CILANTRO, AND DON'T FORGET THAT GLASS OF PREMIUM CUBAN RUM.

# GRILLED VENISON CHOPS

## SERVES 4

## INGREDIENTS

1 cup butter, softened
1 tablespoon shallot, minced
1 tablespoon fresh parsley, minced
2 teaspoons Dijon mustard
4 thick venison chops

## DIRECTIONS

In a medium bowl, combine the butter with the shallot, parsley and mustard. Place on a square of plastic wrap, form into a log and refrigerate until solid.

Place the chops on a hot grill. Give chops a quarter turn at 8 minutes and flip at 12 minutes. Do another quarter turn at 20 minutes and remove from the grill at 32 minutes. Serve with slices of the seasoned butter.

## HENRY SAYS: THIS DISH IS RATHER SIMPLE TO PREPARE, BUT HAS SOME PRETTY SPECTACULAR RESULTS.

# HONEY-GLAZED VENISON ROAST

## SERVES 6–8

## INGREDIENTS

4 stalks celery, cut into thirds
2 medium onions, sliced
3–4 pound venison roast
salt & pepper to taste
6 strips thick-cut bacon
3 cups baby carrots
1 pound baby red potatoes
½ cup craisins
3 teaspoons garlic, minced
1½ cups chicken stock
1½ cups white wine
1 cup balsamic vinegar
1½ cups honey

## DIRECTIONS

Place celery and half of the onions in the bottom of a 4 to 5 quart slow cooker to form a rack. Season the roast with salt and pepper to taste and place in the slow cooker on the celery and onions. Drape the bacon strips over the roast. Place the carrots, potatoes, craisins and remaining onions around the roast. Mix together the garlic, chicken stock, wine, vinegar and 1 cup of the honey. Pour over the venison. Cover and cook on low 8 to 10 hours.

Remove 2 cups of the cooking liquid and place in a medium saucepan. Whisk in the remaining ½ cup honey and bring to a boil over high heat. Lower heat to medium and reduce by half, stirring constantly. Serve with the roast and vegetables.

## HENRY SAYS: AND FOR DESSERT, A DECADENT CHOCOLATE CAKE WITH RASPBERRY FILLING PERHAPS?

# MARINATED VENISON ROAST

## SERVES 4–6

### INGREDIENTS
3 pounds venison roast

### MARINADE
4 cups dry red wine
4 peppercorns, crushed
10 fresh celery leaves, chopped
2 cloves garlic, crushed
2 celery stalks, finely chopped
3 whole cloves
1 sprig thyme
1 sprig parsley
¼ teaspoon sea salt

### DIRECTIONS
Place the venison in an extra-large sealable plastic bag. Mix the marinade ingredients in a medium bowl. Pour over the venison and seal the bag, pushing out as much air as possible. Place the bag in a bowl and refrigerate for at least 24 hours, turning every 8 hours.

Preheat oven to 350 degrees. Remove the roast from the marinade and pat dry with paper towels. Strain and reserve the marinade, discarding the vegetables.

Rub the roast with olive oil and season lightly with salt and pepper. Heat a Dutch oven over medium-high heat. Add 3 tablespoons olive oil and brown the roast on all sides. Transfer the roast to a baking dish. Pour the marinade over the roast, cover and place in the oven. Roast for 2½ hours. Remove from the oven and let stand 15 minutes before slicing.

HENRY SAYS: YOU MAY LIKE TO ADD B-SIZED POTATOES AND BABY CARROTS TO THE PAN FOR THE LAST HALF HOUR OF ROASTING TIME—AN EASY WAY TO PREPARE YOUR VEGETABLES. ALSO, THICKEN THE PAN JUICES FOR A WONDERFUL GRAVY.

# MUSTARD-GLAZED VENISON TENDERLOIN

## SERVES 3–4

## INGREDIENTS

¼ cup brown sugar
2 tablespoons butter, softened
¼ cup whole-grain mustard
¼ teaspoon granulated garlic
1 large onion, thinly sliced
1 pound venison tenderloin
6 fresh basil leaves

## DIRECTIONS

Preheat oven to 400 degrees. In a medium bowl, combine the brown sugar, butter, mustard and granulated garlic.

Place a sheet of heavy duty aluminum foil large enough to accommodate the venison on a flat surface. Spray the foil with cooking spray. Layer the onions down the center and place the venison on top of the onions. Coat the venison with half of the brown sugar/mustard mixture.

Bring the long edges of the foil together and double fold. Do the same on the ends. Place the packet on a baking sheet. Place in the oven. Immediately reduce heat to 350 degrees and bake for 20 to 25 minutes, or until the internal temperature reads 130 degrees.

Remove the venison from the oven and carefully open by cutting the top with a sharp knife. Heat oven to broil (400–425 degrees). Spread remaining brown sugar/mustard mixture on the venison and place in the oven for 1 to 3 minutes, or until a light crust forms on top. Remove from the oven and let rest for 10 minutes before slicing. Garnish with fresh basil leaves.

## HENRY SAYS: THIS RECIPE WORKS EQUALLY WELL WITH VENISON BACK STRAP.

# NUTMEG AND CUMIN ENCRUSTED VENISON LOIN CHOPS

## SERVES 4

## INGREDIENTS

1 cup Panko bread crumbs
½ teaspoon ground cumin
½ teaspoon ground nutmeg
½ teaspoon sea salt
¼ teaspoon white pepper
1 large egg, beaten
½ cup whole-grain mustard
8 thinly sliced venison loin chops
4 tablespoons olive oil

## DIRECTIONS

In a shallow bowl, combine the bread crumbs, cumin, nutmeg, salt and pepper. In another bowl, whisk together the egg and mustard. Dip the venison chops in the egg mixture and then dredge in the bread crumb mixture.

Heat a large non-stick skillet over medium heat. Add 2 tablespoons olive oil and 4 venison chops. Brown 3 to 4 minutes on each side. Keep warm in a 225 degree oven while browning the remaining chops. Plate 2 chops per serving.

## HENRY SAYS: THE PERFECT ACCOMPANIMENT FOR THESE CHOPS IS SWEET AND SOUR RED CABBAGE.

# PROSCIUTTO-WRAPPED VENISON TENDERLOIN

## SERVES 6–8

## INGREDIENTS

12 slices prosciutto
3 1½–2 pound venison tenderloins
1 medium onion, thinly sliced
6 sun-dried tomatoes, drained and finely sliced
1 clove garlic, minced
2 tablespoons butter, melted

## DIRECTIONS

Preheat oven to 425 degrees.

Place 3 sheets of wax paper on 3 small baking pans. Place 4 slices of prosciutto on each piece of paper, overlapping slightly. Cut each tenderloin in half across the middle and lay side-by-side on the prosciutto to form a uniform log.

Arrange ⅓ of the onion slices, tomatoes and garlic on each tenderloin. Use the wax paper to tightly roll the venison, prosciutto and vegetables together.

Transfer to a non-stick baking pan and carefully unroll and remove the wax paper. Brush with the melted butter and bake 15 to 20 minutes or until the prosciutto begins to brown and the internal temperature of the venison reaches 120 degrees. Let stand for 10 minutes before slicing.

## HENRY SAYS: SERVE THESE MEDALLIONS OF VENISON WITH A CRISP SALAD, FRESHLY BAKED BREAD, STEAMED VEGETABLES, POLENTA AND A ROBUST RED WINE. YOU'LL AMAZE YOUR GUESTS WITH YOUR CULINARY PROWESS.

# RACK OF VENISON

## SERVES 2–4

## INGREDIENTS
1 8-bone rack of venison
2 tablespoons lemon juice

## DRY RUB
1 teaspoon oregano, crushed
½ teaspoon marjoram, crushed
¼ teaspoon sea salt
¼ teaspoon granulated garlic
¼ teaspoon dried lemon peel, ground
¼ teaspoon dried orange peel, ground
⅛ teaspoon white pepper
⅛ teaspoon black pepper

## DIRECTIONS
Mix together all dry rub ingredients in a food processor. Process for 10 seconds.

Moisten the venison rack with lemon juice and dust with the dry rub. Cover and let sit for 30 minutes. Heat a gas or charcoal grill to medium-high. Cook the venison for 3 minutes on a side. Place venison in a baking dish and roast in a 350 degree oven for 15 minutes. Let the venison sit loosely covered for 10 minutes before carving.

## HENRY SAYS: USE THE SAME DRY RUB ON CHICKEN OR LAMB. FOR ADDED FLAVOR, BASTE DURING BAKING WITH GARLIC BUTTER AND LEMON JUICE.

# ROAST LEG OF VENISON

## SERVES 8

## INGREDIENTS
1 boneless leg of venison
10 strips thick-cut bacon

## MARINADE
4 cups red wine
2 cups red wine vinegar
1 tablespoon salt
½ teaspoon black pepper
½ teaspoon thyme
2 medium onions, sliced
3 carrots, cut into 3 inch pieces
4 tablespoons vegetable oil
1 tablespoon garlic, minced

## DIRECTIONS
Mix all marinade ingredients in a container that will also hold the venison and will fit in your refrigerator.

Place venison in marinade and hold down with a non-reactive plate held in place with a plastic bottle filled with water. Marinate 3 to 4 days, turning twice a day.

Preheat oven to 350 degrees. Remove venison from marinade and wipe dry. Wrap the venison with the bacon strips held in place with toothpicks if necessary and place on a rack in a roasting pan. Allowing 15 to 18 minutes per pound of meat, cook until internal temperature reaches 140 degrees.

## HENRY SAYS: IF YOU REALLY WANT TO IMPRESS YOUR FRIENDS, CARVE THIS AT THE TABLE.

# SOUTHWESTERN VENISON

## SERVES 4–6

## INGREDIENTS

2 pounds venison, cut into 1½ inch cubes
1 medium onion, chopped
2 cloves garlic, minced
¼ teaspoon black pepper
½ teaspoon salt
1½ tablespoons mild chili powder
1 chicken bouillon cube, crushed and mixed with the juice from the tomatoes
1 15 ounce can stewed tomatoes, drain and save the juice
1 15 ounce can kidney beans

## DIRECTIONS

Place the venison in a large cast iron or heavy-duty Dutch oven. Cover with the onion, garlic, pepper, salt and chili powder. Add the chicken bouillon in the tomato juice and the tomatoes, stirring to incorporate all of the ingredients.

Simmer over low heat for 3 hours, or until the venison is tender. Add wine or beer if more liquid is needed. Stir in the beans and heat for an additional 20 minutes. Serve over rice or thick slices of sourdough bread.

## HENRY SAYS: A HEARTY BEER IS A PARTICULARLY GOOD ACCOMPANIMENT TO THIS DISH.

# STOVETOP VENISON ROAST

## SERVES 6–8

## INGREDIENTS
4 pound venison roast, deboned, rolled and tied
¼ cup flour
2 tablespoons butter
3 tablespoons olive oil
2 envelopes onion soup mix
1½ cups apple cider
½ teaspoon mustard seed
3 stalks celery, cut into 2 inch pieces
6 carrots, cut into 2 inch pieces
4 parsnips, peeled and cut into 1 inch dice

## DIRECTIONS
Dust the roast with the flour. Heat the butter and olive oil in a large Dutch oven over medium heat. Add the roast and brown on all sides.

Combine the soup mix with the apple cider and mustard seed and pour over the roast. Cover, reduce heat to low and cook for 2 hours.

Add the celery, carrots and parsnips. Cover and cook an additional 40 minutes, or until the vegetables are tender. Transfer the roast to a platter. Remove the string and decorate the platter with vegetables. Strain the cooking liquid and serve as a sauce on the side.

## HENRY SAYS: ALL YOU REALLY NEED WITH THIS IS A LOAF OF YOUR FAVORITE BREAD.

# SWEDISH VENISON STEAK

## SERVES 6–8

## INGREDIENTS

3 pounds venison, cut into serving pieces and seasoned with salt and pepper
1 teaspoon dill weed
1 large onion, sliced
2 large carrots, sliced
3 cups beef consommé
¼ cup flour
½ cup white wine
1 cup sour cream
1 tablespoon fresh dill, minced

## DIRECTIONS

Place venison in a slow cooker. Add the dill weed, onion, carrots and consommé. Cover and cook on low 5 to 6 hours, or until tender.

Remove the venison to a covered plate. Increase the heat to high. Mix the flour and wine. Add to the cooking liquid in the slow cooker, stirring constantly until thickened. Turn heat off and stir in the sour cream and fresh dill. Serve the sauce over the venison with mashed potatoes or buttered noodles.

## HENRY SAYS: TRY ADDING A SIDE OF PICKLED GHERKINS AND CRANBERRY SAUCE OR THE MORE TRADITIONAL LINGONBERRY SAUCE.

# VENISON MEDITERRANEAN

## SERVES 8

## INGREDIENTS

3 pounds venison loin, cut into 1 inch cubes
8 12 inch wooden skewers

## MARINADE

¼ cup red wine vinegar
¼ cup lemon juice
½ cup olive oil
1 medium onion, minced
4 cloves garlic, minced
1 teaspoon ground cumin
1 tablespoon dry oregano
1 tablespoon dry mint

## DIRECTIONS

In a large bowl, mix all marinade ingredients. Add the venison and mix well. Cover and refrigerate for at least 24 hours.

Soak the skewers in water for ½ hour. Divide meat into 8 equal portions and thread on skewers leaving a small space between the pieces of meat. Cook on a gas grill set at medium-high or a very hot charcoal grill. Turn often and brush with marinade until venison is well browned.

HENRY SAYS: SERVE WITH LEMON WEDGES AND A SAUCE MADE WITH 2 CUPS GREEK YOGHURT, 2 TABLESPOONS MINCED FRESH OREGANO, 2 TABLESPOONS MINCED FRESH ROSEMARY, 1 TEASPOON SEA SALT AND 1 TEASPOON FRESHLY GROUND BLACK PEPPER. AND DON'T FORGET THE RODITIS!

# VENISON PEPPER STEAK

## SERVES 4–6

## INGREDIENTS

3 tablespoons butter
3 tablespoons vegetable oil
2 pounds venison steak, cut into long narrow strips
2 green pepper, seeded and cut into 1 inch strips
2 sweet red peppers, seeded and cut into 1 inch strips
2 onions, thickly sliced
2 15 ounce cans stewed tomatoes
1 teaspoon seasoned salt
½ teaspoon black pepper

## DIRECTIONS

In a large Dutch oven, heat the butter and oil over medium heat. Add the venison and stir until all sides are browned. Add the remaining ingredients. Reduce heat to low, cover and simmer for 2 hours. Adjust seasoning with additional salt and pepper and use 1 tablespoon brown sugar to reduce acidity if required. Serve with mashed potatoes.

HENRY SAYS: THIS IS SUCH AN EASY DISH TO PREPARE, BUT YOUR FAMILY AND FRIENDS WILL THINK YOU SLAVED OVER THE STOVE ALL AFTERNOON.

# VENISON SAUERBRATEN

## SERVES 6–8

## INGREDIENTS
4 pounds venison roast

## MARINADE
1 cup dry red wine
1 cup red wine vinegar
2 cups cranberry juice
1 spice bag with 1 teaspoon pickling spice,
   2 bay leaves, 6 whole cloves and
   10 peppercorns
1 medium onion, sliced

## BRAISING LIQUID
¼ pound butter
¼ pound bacon, chopped
1 cup onion, chopped
1 cup celery, chopped
1 cup carrot, chopped
10 peppercorns, crushed
1 cup dry red wine
½ cup red wine vinegar
2 cups beef stock

## SAUCE FINISH
½ cup Knorr Demi-glace sauce mix
1 cup braising liquid
1 cup ginger snap cookies, finely chopped
   (10 to 12 cookies)
1 cup cream sherry

## DIRECTIONS
To make the marinade, bring cranberry juice to a boil in a 1 quart saucepan. Add spice bag, remove from the heat and allow to cool.

Place venison roast in a 2½ gallon Ziploc bag. Add onions, cooled cranberry juice with the spice bag, red wine and red wine vinegar. Place bag in large bowl or deep pan and refrigerate for at least 2 to 3 days. Rotate and flip the bag 3 times each day.

Preheat oven to 325 degrees.

Remove the roast from the marinade. Wipe off excess moisture and place on a holding tray. Strain marinade, discarding the vegetables and spice bag, reserving the liquid.

In a large, deep Dutch oven, melt the butter and brown the roast on all sides. Remove the venison to a holding tray. Add the bacon to the Dutch oven, stir and cook 3 to 4 minutes. Remove and reserve the bacon for the sauce. Add the celery, carrot and onion to the Dutch oven, stirring and cooking for 5 minutes. Return the venison to the Dutch oven. Add the peppercorns, wine, red wine vinegar and stock. Bring to a boil, cover and place in the oven for 2 to 3 hours or until venison is fork tender. Remove from the oven, uncover and cool to room temperature. Strain and discard the vegetables. Reserve the strained braising liquid. Refrigerate the venison and liquid overnight.

Remove excess fat from the surface of the braising liquid. Remove venison, slice and arrange in a decorative baking/serving dish. Heat 1 cup of the braising liquid over medium heat. Whisk in the sauce mix, gingersnaps and sherry, whisking until the sauce thickens. Spoon sauce over the venison and warm in a 150 degree oven for 15 to 20 minutes.

# VENISON WITH BEER AND DILL

## SERVES 4–6

### INGREDIENTS

3 pounds venison roast
1 tablespoon olive oil
¼ teaspoon salt
¼ teaspoon pepper
3 tablespoons flour
3 tablespoons olive oil
3 medium onions, thinly sliced
2 cloves garlic, minced
2 cups dark beer
1 teaspoon brown sugar
1 teaspoon seasoned salt
2 tablespoons fresh dill, chopped
6 carrots, cut to fit in the bottom of the Dutch oven

### DIRECTIONS

Rub the roast with 1 tablespoon olive oil, season with salt and pepper and dust with flour.

Heat 3 tablespoons olive oil in a large Dutch oven over medium heat. Quickly brown the roast on all sides. Remove the roast and add the onions and garlic and stir-fry for 3 minutes. Stir in the beer, brown sugar, seasoned salt and dill.

Arrange the carrots on the bottom of the Dutch oven to form a rack for the roast. Place the roast on the carrots, cover and reduce the heat to low. Cook for 2 hours. Remove the roast to a warm platter and let rest for 15 minutes before slicing.

Strain cooking liquid into a saucepan. Bring to a boil and reduce by half.

## HENRY SAYS: SERVE WITH A SIMPLE GREEN SALAD, OVEN BROWNED POTATOES, STEAMED ASPARAGUS AND, FOR DESSERT, LEMON GELATO. OH, AND DON'T FORGET THE BEER.

# VENISON WITH MUSHROOM GRAVY

## SERVES 6

## INGREDIENTS

3 pounds venison, cut into 6 pieces
1 package onion soup mix
½ cup water
2 cans cream of mushroom soup
1 clove garlic, minced
¼ teaspoon pepper
¼ teaspoon salt
1 teaspoon brown sugar
2 cups fresh mushrooms, washed and sliced

## DIRECTIONS

Place the venison in a large Dutch oven. Mix all remaining ingredients, except the mushrooms, in a medium bowl and pour over the venison. Bring to a slow boil over medium heat. Reduce heat to low. Cover and simmer for 2 hours, or until venison is tender. Add water as necessary.

Add the mushrooms and simmer an additional 15 minutes. Serve with boiled potatoes.

## HENRY SAYS: MUSHROOMS ARE KNOWN AS THE "MEAT" OF THE VEGETABLE WORLD.

# MISCELLANEOUS

# VENISON STUFFED GREEN PEPPERS

## SERVES 6

### INGREDIENTS

½ pound ground venison
½ pound bulk sweet Italian sausage
½ pound bulk mild Italian sausage
1 medium onion, peeled, sliced and chopped
½ cup cooked wild rice
½ cup ricotta cheese
6 green bell peppers, tops, seeds and white membrane removed
1 18 ounce can Italian vegetable soup
1 cup chicken stock
6 slices mozzarella cheese

### DIRECTIONS

Preheat oven to 325 degrees. Coat a deep covered Dutch oven with non-stick spray.

In a medium bowl, mix the venison, sausages, onion, wild rice and ricotta cheese. Stuff each pepper with an equal portion of this mixture and arrange them in the Dutch oven.

Pour the soup and the chicken stock over the peppers and top each with a slice of mozzarella. Bake for 40 to 50 minutes or until internal temperature reaches 160 degrees.

## HENRY SAYS: THIS IS THE PERFECT DISH FOR A CASUAL BUFFET DINNER.

# VENISON SHEPHERD'S PIE

## SERVES 4–6

## INGREDIENTS
½ pound ground venison
½ pound sweet Italian sausage
1 can vegetable soup
1 clove garlic, minced (about 1 teaspoon)
1 15 ounce can sweet peas, drained
1 15 ounce can corn, drained
¼ teaspoon black pepper
1 package dehydrated mashed potatoes, prepared with milk and butter

## DIRECTIONS
Preheat oven to 350 degrees. Remove the casing from the Italian sausage and mix with the venison.

In a large cast iron skillet or Dutch oven, brown the venison/sausage mixture. Stir in the soup, garlic, peas, corn and pepper. Top with a layer of the mashed potatoes.

Bake for 30 to 40 minutes or until the potatoes are browned.

## HENRY SAYS: SERVE WITH A SIMPLE SALAD AND A CRISP WHITE WINE.

# VENISON RIBS WITH SAUERKRAUT

## SERVES 4–6

## INGREDIENTS

3 pounds venison ribs, trimmed of any fat and cut into serving pieces
1 teaspoon salt
½ teaspoon white pepper
2 pounds fresh sauerkraut, drained and rinsed under cold water
2 large carrots, shredded
1 large onion, sliced and cut in half
1 Granny Smith apple, cored and shredded
1 8 ounce bottle V-8 Juice
2 tablespoons honey
2 teaspoons caraway seeds (optional)

## DIRECTIONS

Season the ribs with salt and pepper and place in a deep Dutch oven. Combine the remaining ingredients in a large bowl. Pour over the ribs. Cover and bake for 1½ hours. Remove the cover and bake until tender, approximately another 1½ hours.

# HENRY SAYS: IF YOU CUT THESE RIBS INTO SMALL PORTIONS, THEY MAKE A WONDERFUL APPETIZER.

# VENISON QUICHE

## SERVES 4–6

## INGREDIENTS

1 9 inch pie shell
3 tablespoons butter
1 pound ground venison
4 strips pre-cooked bacon, crumbled
3 tablespoons chives, minced
¾ cup fresh mushrooms, sliced
1 cup Swiss cheese, grated
2 eggs
1 cup heavy cream
⅛ teaspoon granulated garlic
⅛ teaspoon nutmeg
¼ teaspoon salt
⅛ teaspoon white pepper

## DIRECTIONS

Preheat oven to 425 degrees. Pre-bake the pie shell for 5 minutes. Remove from the oven and cool. Reduce oven temperature to 400 degrees.

In a large skillet, melt the butter over medium heat. Add the venison and cook until browned, stirring constantly. Transfer the venison to the pie shell. Distribute the bacon and chives over the venison followed by the mushrooms and cheese.

In a medium bowl, beat together the eggs and cream. Add the granulated garlic, nutmeg, salt and pepper, and mix well.

Place the pie shell on a baking tray. Pour the egg mixture into the pie shell and place in the oven. Bake for 25 to 30 minutes, or until top begins to brown. Let stand for 15 minutes before slicing.

## HENRY SAYS: SERVE WITH FRESH FRUIT AND CINNAMON TOAST.

# VENISON PICCATA

## SERVES 4

### INGREDIENTS

1 cup cracker crumbs
1 egg, beaten with 1 tablespoon water
8 pieces boneless venison, sliced ¼ inch thick and pounded thin
¼ pound unsalted butter
1 teaspoon garlic, minced
1 shallot, minced
1 teaspoon parsley
1 tablespoon Worcestershire sauce
1 tablespoon capers
1 tablespoon fresh lemon juice
¼ cup white wine

### DIRECTIONS

In a food processor fitted with a stainless steel blade, pulse chop the cracker crumbs to produce an almost flour-like product.

Dip the venison cutlet in the beaten egg, then the cracker crumbs, coating both sides. Gently shake off excess cracker crumbs and place on a staging tray.

In a heavy skillet, melt half the butter over medium heat and quickly sauté the venison cutlets until they are golden brown on each side, 30 seconds to 1 minute per side. Remove to a paper towel lined pan and hold in a warm oven.

With a paper towel, carefully remove any cracker crumbs from the sauté pan. Reduce heat to low. Melt the remaining butter and quickly sauté the shallot and garlic. Stir in the parsley, Worcestershire sauce, capers, lemon juice and white wine. Increase heat to medium, bring to a boil and turn off heat.

Plate 2 venison cutlets per person. Spoon 1 tablespoon of sauce over each cutlet and serve with steamed vegetables.

## HENRY SAYS: A GRATING OF FRESH PARMESAN CHEESE BUMPS UP THE FLAVOR PROFILE OF THIS DISH.

# VENISON MUFFINS

## SERVES 12

### INGREDIENTS

1½ pounds ground venison
1½ pounds bulk pork sausage
⅓ cup ketchup
1 egg, beaten
½ cup seasoned bread crumbs
¼ teaspoon granulated garlic
¼ teaspoon white pepper
⅓ cup white cheddar cheese, grated
1 teaspoon smoked paprika
1 can jellied cranberry sauce, cut into 12 equal portions
1 package four cheese mashed potatoes, prepared with milk and 1 tablespoon butter

### DIRECTIONS

Preheat oven to 325 degrees. Coat the bottom and sides of 12 large muffin cups with non-stick spray.

In a large bowl, mix together the venison, sausage, ketchup, egg, bread crumbs, granulated garlic, pepper, cheese and paprika. Blend well. Divide into 12 equal portions and press lightly into muffin cups. Place a slice of cranberry sauce on the meat mixture and top with the mashed potatoes.

Bake until the potatoes are golden brown and the meat reaches 150 degrees. Remove from the oven and let sit 15 minutes before serving.

## HENRY SAYS: LEFTOVERS CAN BE FROZEN INDIVIDUALLY FOR A QUICK MEAL ON THE GO.

# VENISON MINCEMEAT

## SERVES 2 9 INCH PIES

### INGREDIENTS
1 pound venison, coarsely chopped
2 cups apples, peeled, cored and finely diced
2 cups apple cider
1 cup currants
1 cup golden raisins
1 cup craisins
zest 1 lemon
zest 1 orange
⅓ cup brown sugar
¼ cup white sugar
½ teaspoon salt
½ teaspoon cinnamon
¼ teaspoon ground cloves
¼ teaspoon allspice
½ cup candied citron, finely chopped
1 cup brandy

### DIRECTIONS
In a heavy stockpot, combine the venison, apples and cider. Bring to a low boil over medium-high heat. Stir in the remaining ingredients except for the brandy. Reduce heat to low. Simmer 1 hour, stirring occasionally. Remove from the heat and carefully stir in the brandy.

## HENRY SAYS: THIS IS A GREAT WAY TO USE SMALL PIECES OF VENISON THAT END UP IN THE FREEZER.

# VENISON MAC

## SERVES 6

## INGREDIENTS

3 tablespoons olive oil
1½ pounds ground venison
½ pound bulk pork sausage
1 medium onion, chopped
2 stalks celery, thinly sliced
1 green pepper, seeded, sliced and chopped
1 teaspoon garlic, chopped
¼ teaspoon nutmeg
¼ teaspoon salt
¼ teaspoon pepper
½ teaspoon oregano
1 small can sliced black olives
2 15 ounce cans stewed tomatoes, chopped
1 pound elbow macaroni, cooked according to package directions
½ pound grated mozzarella cheese

## DIRECTIONS

Preheat oven to 350 degrees.

In a large Dutch oven, heat the olive oil over medium heat and brown the venison and pork sausage. Stir in the onion, celery, green pepper and garlic. Cook until the onions are translucent.

Mix in the nutmeg, salt, pepper, oregano and black olives. Add the stewed tomatoes and simmer for 30 minutes. Mix in the cooked macaroni and 1 cup of the cheese.

Transfer to a greased baking dish and bake for 25 minutes. Top with the remaining cheese and bake an additional 15 to 20 minutes until cheese is melted and begins to brown.

## HENRY SAYS: THIS DISH SHOULD APPEAL TO ALL AGES AND CAN BE PREPARED AHEAD (UP TO THE POINT OF BAKING) SO YOU CAN SPEND YOUR TIME ENJOYING YOUR FAMILY AND FRIENDS.

# VENISON LASAGNA

## SERVES 6–8

## INGREDIENTS

2 tablespoons olive oil
2 pounds ground venison
1 pound bulk Italian sausage
1 large onion, finely chopped
1 clove garlic, minced
1 tablespoon brown sugar
2 jars pasta sauce
½ tablespoon oregano
12 lasagna noodles, cooked
1 pound mozzarella cheese, shredded
15 ounces ricotta cheese
1½ cups Parmesan cheese
1 bayleaf
1 pound ground venison
4 strips pre-cooked bacon, shredded
1 egg
¼ teaspoon seasoned salt
¼ teaspoon white pepper

## DIRECTIONS

In a large saucepan, heat the oil over medium heat. Add the venison and sausage, and stir to combine and brown. Add the onion, garlic, brown sugar, pasta sauce and oregano. Stir and simmer for 20 to 30 minutes. Adjust seasoning to taste with salt and pepper.

Preheat oven to 325 degrees. Butter the bottom and sides of a 9x13 inch baking dish. Cover the bottom with 3 of the noodles. Spread a layer of ricotta, a layer of sauce, a layer of mozzarella and another layer of noodles. Repeat these layers 2 more times. Top with a layer of sauce and mozzarella cheese. Bake for 60 minutes. Remove from the oven and let stand 15 minutes before serving.

## HENRY SAYS: LOAF OF BREAD, A GLASS OF WINE ANYONE?

# VENISON COTTAGE PIE

## SERVES 4–6

### INGREDIENTS

1 pound venison, cut into 1 inch pieces
¼ cup flour, seasoned with 1 teaspoon seasoned salt and ¼ teaspoon pepper
⅓ cup olive oil
6 strips thick-cut bacon, coarsely chopped
1 large onion, sliced and diced
3 stalks celery, thinly sliced
2 cups chicken stock
1 12 ounce can pumpkin
2 10 ounce bags frozen mixed vegetables
1 package mashed potatoes, prepared with milk and 2 tablespoons butter

### DIRECTIONS

Preheat oven to 350 degrees.

Dust venison with the seasoned flour. Heat the oil in a heavy Dutch oven over medium-high heat. Add the venison and stir to brown on all sides. Stir in the bacon, onions, celery, chicken stock, pumpkin and vegetables.

Cover and reduce heat to low. Simmer for 1 hour. Transfer the venison mixture to a 2-quart casserole. Cover completely with the mashed potatoes. Dot the top of the mashed potatoes with thin slices of butter. Bake for 30 minutes or until the potatoes are browned.

## HENRY SAYS: ALL THIS DISH NEEDS IS A SALAD, A LOAF OF BREAD AND A GLASS OF WINE.

# VENISON BREAKFAST RING

## SERVES 8–10

## INGREDIENTS
1 pound ground venison
1 pound bulk sweet Italian sausage
1 cup apples, peeled and chopped
1 small onion, minced
2 stalks celery, sliced and finely chopped
1½ cup Panko bread crumbs
2 eggs
½ cup cream

## DIRECTIONS
Preheat oven to 325 degrees.

In a large bowl, combine the venison, sausage, apples, onion, celery and bread crumbs. Mix well. Beat the eggs with the cream and blend into the meat mixture.

Pack into a greased 6 cup ring mold. Unmold onto a shallow baking pan. Bake 1 hour or until internal temperature reaches 160 degrees.

## HENRY SAYS: USE THIS DISH AS THE CENTERPIECE FOR A BREAKFAST BUFFET SERVED ALONGSIDE SCRAMBLED EGGS, HASH BROWNS AND FRENCH TOAST, PANCAKES OR WAFFLES.

# VENISON AND YELLOW SQUASH CASSEROLE

## SERVES 6–8

## INGREDIENTS

1 pound large rotelle pasta, cooked according to package directions
3 tablespoons butter
1½ pounds ground venison
½ pound bulk pork sausage
1 medium onion, sliced and chopped
1 tablespoon smoked paprika
½ teaspoon garlic salt
¼ teaspoon pepper
¼ teaspoon nutmeg
9 strips pre-cooked bacon, crumbled
2 packages frozen, cubed yellow squash, thawed
½ cup seasoned bread crumbs mixed with ¼ cup Parmesan cheese
1 12 ounce jar your favorite pasta sauce
1 16 ounce package grated white cheese blend

## DIRECTIONS

Preheat oven to 350 degrees. Lightly coat a 3 to 4 quart baking dish with non-stick spray.

In a large sauté pan, melt the butter over medium heat. Add the venison, pork sausage and onion. Stir to combine and sauce until browned, about 10 minutes. Stir in the paprika, garlic salt, pepper and nutmeg.

Divide the pasta, venison mixture, bacon, squash, bread crumbs, pasta sauce and cheese blend into 3 equal and separate portions. Layer the ingredients in this order 3 times in the baking dish. Bake for 20 to 30 minutes or until cheese is melted and top is browned.

## HENRY SAYS: TRY THIS DISH WITH A BOTTLE OF CABERNET OR ZINFANDEL.

# VENISON AND WILD RICE CASSEROLE

## SERVES 4–6

## INGREDIENTS
1 pound venison steak, cut into ½ inch cubes
½ cup flour, seasoned with ¼ teaspoon salt and ¼ teaspoon pepper
⅓ cup olive oil
8 strips pre-cooked bacon, cut into ½ inch pieces
1 cup fresh mushrooms, sliced
1 cup celery, sliced
½ cup onion, minced
½ cup craisins
¼ teaspoon celery salt
¼ teaspoon granulated garlic
¼ teaspoon black pepper
¼ teaspoon dehydrated onion
1 can cream of mushroom soup
3 cups cooked wild rice
3 large eggs, beaten
1 cup white cheddar cheese, shredded

## DIRECTIONS
Preheat oven to 350 degrees.

Dust the venison with the seasoned flour. Heat the olive oil over medium heat in a large sauté pan and brown the venison in batches. Transfer the venison to a large bowl and add the bacon.

Add the mushrooms, celery, onions and craisins to the sauté pan and stir until the onions are wilted. Stir in the spices and soup and add to the venison mixture. Fold the wild rice into the venison mixture and then the beaten eggs.

Transfer the entire mixture to a large buttered baking dish, top with the cheese and bake for 1 to 1½ hours.

## HENRY SAYS: THE FIRST CASSEROLE RECIPES IN THE LATE 1800'S CONSISTED OF RICE THAT WAS POUNDED, PRESSED, AND FILLED WITH A SAVOURY MIXTURE OF MEATS. WE'VE MADE A LOT OF PROGRESS SINCE THEN.

# VENISON AND BLACK BEAN SUPPER

## SERVES 6–8

## INGREDIENTS

4 medium onions, peeled
1 tablespoon butter
1 tablespoon olive oil
1½ pounds ground venison
1 15 ounce can black beans, drained
1 sweet red bell pepper, diced
2 tablespoons smoked paprika
1 teaspoon granulated garlic
2 cups chicken stock
2 tablespoons butter
8 cups fresh spinach, washed and cut into 1 inch ribbons (discard the stems)

## DIRECTIONS

Cut onions in quarters and place on a non-stick baking sheet. Top each with a thin slice of butter. Roast in a 325 degree oven for 15 to 20 minutes, or until golden brown. Set aside.

In a large sauté pan, heat 1 tablespoon butter and olive oil over medium heat. Add the venison and sauté for 5 minutes, stirring constantly. Add the beans, red bell pepper, paprika, granulated garlic and chicken stock. Stir well. Cover and reduce heat to low.

In a large skillet, melt 2 tablespoons butter over low heat. Slowly add the spinach and cook until completely wilted. Drain excess liquid and add the venison and bean mixture. Add the baked onions and toss lightly.

## HENRY SAYS: ADD A LOAF OR TWO OF CRUSTY SOURDOUGH BREAD AND BOTTLES OF CRAFT BEER, AND YOU'VE GOT THE PERFECT FALL MEAL.

# JACK'S VENISON STROGANOFF

## SERVES 4–6

## INGREDIENTS

2 tablespoons butter
¼ pound bulk pork sausage
1 pound ground venison
1 small onion, minced
1 teaspoon minced garlic (2 cloves)
1 can cream of mushroom soup
3 tablespoons ketchup
1 tablespoon yellow prepared mustard
1 cup sour cream

## DIRECTIONS

In a large sauté pan, melt the butter over medium heat and brown the pork sausage. Stir in the venison, onion and garlic and sauté until the venison is no longer pink.

Stir in the mushroom soup, ketchup, mustard and sour cream. Cook over low heat until heated through. Serve over buttered noodles or oven-roasted potatoes.

# HENRY SAYS: THIS IS ONE OF THOSE EASY AND FAST MEALS THAT YOU CAN PUT TOGETHER ON THE FLY.

# GROUND VENISON STROGANOFF

## SERVES 6–8

## INGREDIENTS

1½ pounds ground venison
½ pound ground pork
1 egg, lightly beaten
½ teaspoon white pepper
¼ cup Parmesan cheese, grated
¼ teaspoon nutmeg
½ teaspoon salt
2 tablespoons butter
1 medium onion, minced
1 teaspoon minced garlic (2 cloves)
1 can cream of mushroom soup
1 small can sliced mushrooms
3 tablespoons ketchup
1 tablespoon Worcestershire sauce
1 cup sour cream
¼ cup sherry

## DIRECTIONS

In a medium bowl, mix together the venison, pork, egg, pepper, cheese, nutmeg and salt. Form into 8 thick patties.

In a skillet over medium-high heat, brown the patties in the butter. Remove to a covered plate. Add the onion and garlic to the skillet and sauté for 3 minutes. Stir in the mushroom soup, mushrooms, ketchup, Worcestershire sauce, sour cream and sherry. Reduce heat to low.

Place the venison patties back in the skillet, cover and cook for 15 to 20 minutes (do not allow to boil).

## HENRY SAYS: SERVE OVER BUTTERED NOODLES WITH STEAMED ASPARAGUS FOR AN UPSCALE DOWN-HOME MEAL.

# BRAISED VENISON SHANK

## SERVES 4

### INGREDIENTS

8 pieces venison shank, 2 inches thick
1 cup flour, seasoned with ¼ teaspoon salt and ¼ teaspoon pepper
½ cup olive oil
2 large onions, sliced
4 stalks celery, sliced
3 carrots, sliced
½ cup fresh parsley, chopped
1 bottle Cabernet Sauvignon
2 cups beef stock
2 15 ounce cans stewed tomatoes
2 bay leaves
½ cup craisins

### DIRECTIONS

Preheat oven to 400 degrees. Dredge the venison in the seasoned flour and place in one layer on a tray. Heat ¼ cup of the olive oil in a Dutch oven over medium heat. Brown the shanks on all sides, adding oil as needed. As the shanks are browned, remove them to the tray.

Place any remaining olive oil and the onion, celery, carrots and parsley in the Dutch oven. Cook for 12 to 15 minutes, stirring occasionally. Arrange the shanks on top of the vegetables. Add the wine, beef stock, tomatoes, bay leaves and craisins.

Bring to a slight boil over medium heat. Cover and move to the oven. Reduce temperature to 325 degrees and cook for 2½ to 3 hours or until tender. Serve in bowls with the braised vegetables.

## HENRY SAYS: ADD MASHED OR STEAMED POTATOES, FRESH GREEN BEANS WITH PARMESAN CHEESE AND FRESHLY BAKED BREAD, AND YOU CAN EASILY SERVE 8 PEOPLE WITH THIS RECIPE.

# BARBECUED VENISON RIBS

## SERVES 4–8

## INGREDIENTS

3 to 5 pounds venison ribs, trimmed of all fat and cut into serving pieces
olive oil
salt & pepper

## SAUCE

1 cup water
1 large can frozen orange juice concentrate
¼ cup teriyaki sauce
2 tablespoons brown sugar
¼ cup lemon juice
1 teaspoon dry mustard
1 tablespoon garlic, minced
1 cup ketchup
3 tablespoons Worcestershire sauce
1 medium onion, minced
¼ cup sorghum molasses
3 tablespoons chili powder

## DIRECTIONS

Preheat oven to 425 degrees.

In a large saucepan over low heat, combine the water and orange juice concentrate. Stir in the remaining sauce ingredients. Simmer for 20 minutes to develop the flavors. Remove from heat.

Rub ribs with olive oil and season with salt and pepper. Place ribs flat (do not overlap) on a baking pan. Bake for 20 minutes. Turn and bake another 20 minutes. Reduce oven temperature to 250 degrees. Baste ribs with the sauce and continue basting every 20 minutes for 3 to 4 hours or until ribs are tender.

## HENRY SAYS: SERVE WITH GRILLED FRESH VEGETABLES OR ROASTED EARS OF CORN AND TWICE-BAKED POTATOES.

# RECIPE NOTES

# RECIPE NOTES

# RECIPE NOTES

# RECIPE NOTES

# RECIPE NOTES